This is a choice study of t[...]ng scholar and gifted exposi[...] of this chapter, but what he p[...] spiritual riches as we seldom read today. Those who read his earlier book on Romans, *A Passion For God*, hoped he might deal with chapter eight more fully. Here he has done so magnificently, and it will be your great loss not to read it.

Eric Alexander

Ray Ortlund writes as he speaks, clearly and passionately. Here exegetical skill is employed with the practical day-to-day life of the believer always in plain focus. Ortlund is a pastor/scholar who understands the real needs God's people. In dealing with this classic Pauline work (Romans 8) he keeps the Word and Spirit model in view throughout. I heartily commend this valuable work to both pastors and lay people alike. It will serve to get many readers into the truth of this vital chapter in a fresh way while retaining the orthodox understanding of the text throughout.

John H. Armstrong
President, Reformation & Revival Ministries
Carol Stream, Illinois

What is a Christian? How are we to live the Christian life? Where are we going in our Christian pilgrimage? All these are questions which we struggle with almost daily as Christians and all are taken up by Paul in the eighth chapter of the book of Romans. Raymond Ortlund opens up this great chapter in a way which not only shows sensitivity to the text of what Paul was saying, but also great awareness of the needs his Christian readers are facing every day. The overwhelming impact of this study is to fill us again with wonder at the greatness of God and the greatness of the salvation he gives to all who come to him through Christ.

Mark G. Johnston
Grove Chapel, Camberwell

This book on one of the most loved chapters of the Bible should gain attention and careful reading for some important reasons. One, pastoral theology, that is, God's truth as applied by one of God's undershepherds to the eternal interests of God's sheep, found and to be found, constitutes the burden of each chapter. Two, rarely will one find a pastor as keenly informed on the biblical languages, historic theology, current issues, as thoroughly committed to a ministry of the Word in proclamation and print, and as lovingly sensitive to the souls of his parishioners as is the author of this book. Third, truths most offensive to the natural man, yet most salutary and essential for him, find expression that is both plain and eloquent. In a generation when many so-called evangelicals seem soured on the gospel, this is a healthy and encouraging read.

Tom Nettles
Southern Baptist Seminary, Louisville

Some books are filled with practical wisdom but they lack theological depth. Others are theologically rich but they fail to speak to the common person. Ray Ortlund in his exposition of Romans 8 has succeeded in weaving together both truth and application, both theology and the realities of everyday life. He shows that Romans 8 speaks to many of our deepest needs, such as the need for forgiveness, power, assurance, and security.

Tom Schreiner
Southern Baptist Seminary, Louisville

I can't think of anyone more qualified than Ray Ortlund to take us on spiritual pilgrimage through Romans 8. For years I have recommended his book, *A Passion for God*, a collection of prayers and meditations on Paul's epistle to the Romans. Ray has now focused his remarkable exegetical and pastoral skills on Romans 8, the crown jewel of the most influential book ever written. There is meat for the hungry soul here. There is refreshing water for the thirsty spirit. Ray's confidence in the power of the Spirit-energized Word of God shows forth on every page of this wonderful, Christ-exalting study of Romans 8. Get it. Then let it get you!

Sam Storms
Wheaton College

SUPERNATURAL LIVING FOR NATURAL PEOPLE

Studies in Romans 8

Raymond C. Ortlund, Jr.

Christian Focus

© Raymond C Ortlund, Jr.

ISBN 1 85792 694 3

Published in 2001 by
Christian Focus Publications,
Geanies House, Fearn,
Ross-shire, IV20 1TW, Great Britain

Cover design by Owen Daily

Printed and bound in Great Britain by
The Guernsey Press Co. Ltd., Guernsey, Channel Islands

Contents

For Tony and Marlene

'I thank my God upon every remembrance of you'
Philippians 1:3

Preface

One simple conviction energizes this book as it goes out into the world. It is this. The urgent need of the hour is the eternal Word of God coming home to our hearts with fresh power through the Holy Spirit. Paul's letter to the Romans has the potential to transform the church in our generation, as it has in the past. And we *need* revival. We need a new beginning, according to the Word of God. We need 'times of refreshing from the presence of the Lord' (Acts 3:19). And how will we receive the Holy Spirit, except by believing God's Word (Galatians 3:2, 5)?

Chapter 8 of Romans is powerful for renewal in God. It opens up to us the certainty of our peace with God, the ministries of the Spirit, the urgency of personal reformation, the incomparable glory of our eternal inheritance, the inexorable power of God's goodness at work in our daily lives and the invincibility of his loving intentions toward us. 'Come, all you who are thirsty, come to the waters!' (Isaiah 55:1, NIV). Here in Romans 8 there is refreshment enough for dry and thirsty believers!

Do you long for a fresh breakthrough with God? Jesus said, 'It is the Spirit who gives life; the flesh profits nothing; the words that I have spoken to you are spirit and are life' (John 6:63, NASB). Spirit and life! Isn't that what we need, above all else? The flesh profits nothing. What is merely human, however brilliant, will not pull us out of the ditch we have fallen into. But the words that Jesus speaks to us, they are spirit and they are life. I offer you this book as the words of Jesus to you. May you hear his voice. May you be filled with his Spirit. May you be renewed with supernatural life.

I thank Dr. Lane Dennis and Crossway Books for their

kind permission to use the translation of Romans in the
English Standard Version. The ESV will show you in English
the words Paul actually wrote in Romans 8.

I thank Dr. Tom Nettles of Southern Seminary in Louisville
for lending a sharp eye to critique the manuscript. Tom is a
church historian, theologian, loyal follower of Jesus and dear
personal friend.

I thank my brothers on the session of First Presbyterian
Church for authorizing me to set aside the time to complete
this book. And I thank my friends at First Pres for pressing
on for more of Christ with me!

I thank Christian Focus Publications for their collaboration
in making this work available to the world.

I thank my dear wife, Jani, and my fine son, Gavin, for
their encouragement through this task.

The mission of First Presbyterian Church is 'to glorify
God by demonstrating the transforming power of the gospel
of Jesus Christ in our community and around the world.'
Wherever you are, join us in this glorious mission, for God's
greater glory, your richer joy and the salvation of the nations!

Raymond C. Ortlund, Jr.
Augusta, Georgia, USA
December, 2000

Romans 8

¹There is therefore now no condemnation for those who are in Christ Jesus. ²For the law of the Spirit of life has set me free in Christ Jesus from the law of sin and death. ³For God has done what the law, weakened by the flesh, could not do. By sending his own Son in the likeness of sinful flesh and for sin, he condemned sin in the flesh, ⁴in order that the righteous requirement of the law might be fulfilled in us, who walk not according to the flesh but according to the Spirit. ⁵For those who live according to the flesh set their minds on the things of the flesh, but those who live according to the Spirit set their minds on the things of the Spirit. ⁶To set the mind on the flesh is death, but to set the mind on the Spirit is life and peace. ⁷For the mind that is set on the flesh is hostile to God, for it does not submit to God's law; indeed, it cannot. ⁸Those who are in the flesh cannot please God.

⁹You, however, are not in the flesh but in the Spirit, if in fact the Spirit of God dwells in you. Anyone who does not have the Spirit of Christ does not belong to him. ¹⁰But if Christ is in you, although the body is dead because of sin, the Spirit is life because of righteousness. ¹¹If the Spirit of him who raised Jesus from the dead dwells in you, he who raised Christ Jesus from the dead will also give life to your mortal bodies through his Spirit who dwells in you.

¹²So then, brothers, we are debtors, not to the flesh, to live according to the flesh. ¹³For if you live according to the flesh you will die, but if by the Spirit you put to death the deeds of the body, you will live. ¹⁴For all who are led by the Spirit of God are sons of God. ¹⁵For you did not receive the spirit of slavery to fall back into fear, but you have received the Spirit of adoption as sons, by whom we cry, 'Abba! Father!' ¹⁶The Spirit himself bears witness with our spirit that we are children

of God, [17]and if children, then heirs – heirs of God and fellow heirs with Christ, provided we suffer with him in order that we may also be glorified with him.

[18]For I consider that the sufferings of this present time are not worth comparing with the glory that is to be revealed to us. [19]For the creation waits with eager longing for the revealing of the sons of God. [20]For the creation was subjected to futility, not willingly, but because of him who subjected it, in hope [21]that the creation itself will be set free from its bondage to decay and obtain the freedom of the glory of the children of God. [22]For we know that the whole creation has been groaning together in the pains of childbirth until now. [23]And not only the creation, but we ourselves, who have the first fruits of the Spirit, groan inwardly as we wait eagerly for adoption as sons, the redemption of our bodies. [24]For in this hope we were saved. Now hope that is seen is not hope. For who hopes for what he sees? [25]But if we hope for what we do not see, we wait for it with patience.

[26]Likewise the Spirit helps us in our weakness. For we do not know what to pray for as we ought, but the Spirit himself intercedes for us with groanings too deep for words. [27]And he who searches hearts knows what is the mind of the Spirit, because the Spirit intercedes for the saints according to the will of God. [28]And we know that for those who love God all things work together for good, for those who are called according to his purpose. [29]For those whom he foreknew he also predestined to be conformed to the image of his Son, in order that he might be the firstborn among many brothers. [30]And those whom he predestined he also called, and those whom he called he also justified, and those whom he justified he also glorified.

[31]What then shall we say to these things? If God is for us, who can be against us? [32]He who did not spare his own Son but gave him up for us all, how will he not also with him

graciously give us all things? [33]Who shall bring any charge against God's elect? It is God who justifies. [34]Who is to condemn? Christ Jesus is the one who died – more than that, who was raised – who is at the right hand of God, who indeed is interceding for us. [35]Who shall separate us from the love of Christ? Shall tribulation, or distress, or persecution, or famine, or nakedness, or danger, or sword? [36]As it is written,

'For your sake we are being killed all the day long;
we are regarded as sheep to be slaughtered.'

[37]But in all these things we are more than conquerors through him who loved us. [38]For I am sure that neither death nor life, nor angels nor rulers, nor things present nor things to come, nor powers, [39]nor height nor depth, nor anything else in all creation, will be able to separate us from the love of God in Christ Jesus our Lord.

Supernatural Living For Natural People

Chapter One

No Condemnation!

[1] There is therefore now no condemnation for those who are in Christ Jesus. [2] For the law of the Spirit of life has set me free in Christ Jesus from the law of sin and death.

Two great armies clash on the battlefield of life – the people of God and the sins that would defeat them. God's people do not fight as well as they should. Sometimes they even yield to their enemy. But even as the battle rages, well before the promised victory, the Commander of God's army orders a banner to be raised right in the middle of his troops for all to see. The banner reads, 'No condemnation now for those in Christ Jesus!' And that declaration has a remarkable effect upon the people of God. They do not use that assurance as an excuse to defect to the other side. They rejoice in the certainty of their final triumph and are energized to fight on.

Romans 8:1 raises that banner. We look up at it with joy, and it stiffens our resolve not to quit. This verse is like a banner because, in Paul's Greek text, it has no verb. Our English Bible says, '*There is* therefore now no condemnation for those *who are* in Christ Jesus.' But Paul's text is simpler: 'Therefore now no condemnation for those in Christ Jesus!' It is a plain and forceful cry. *No condemnation for sinning, struggling Christians who yearn to be rescued from their Romans 7 frustration and failure!* The only thing that will strengthen you to keep fighting is God's strong assurance of grace.

Romans 8 is one of the richest chapters of the Bible. But what is Paul aiming to accomplish here? What question is he answering? The question driving Romans 8 is this: What can God do for sinners like us, fighting but too often failing? We want to live for the Lord, but every day we betray him. Our hearts cry out with Paul, 'Wretched man that I am! Who will deliver me from this body of death?' (Romans 7:24). So what does God provide for Christians with real problems? Does God have something that can outperform the severe, but ineffective, threats of his law?

Paul has already whispered God's answer to our heartcry earlier in his letter to the Romans: Where sin increased, grace abounded all the more (5:20). We are not under law but under grace (6:14). We now serve God not in the oldness of the letter but in the newness of the Spirit (7:6). And Paul has just shouted for joy, 'Thanks be to God through Jesus Christ our Lord!' (7:25). But how does that actually work out in our lives? What does the gospel have to say to us in the midst of the battle, before the final victory is won, as we struggle and fail – and then fail again?

The key word in Romans 8 is *Spirit*. In chapters 1-7, the word *Spirit* appears only five times. In chapters 9-16 *Spirit* occurs eight times. But here in chapter 8 the word *Spirit* suddenly bursts onto the scene 21 times – usually referring to the Holy Spirit of God – more often than in any other chapter of the entire New Testament.[1]

So God's provision for weak Christians is the Holy Spirit. We do need to get tough on our sinful impulses. But our own self-monitoring cannot actually change us. God's transforming provision for sinning Christians is the sin-expelling Holy Spirit. The reason grace succeeds where law fails is that, while law is empowered by our own good intentions, grace is empowered by the Holy Spirit.

We need a fresh rediscovery of the Holy Spirit in our lives and in our churches today. I am thankful for the honesty of John Stott:

The best way to begin is to stress the importance of our subject by confessing our great need of the power of the Holy Spirit today. We are ashamed of the general worldliness of the church and disturbed by its weakness, its steadily diminishing influence on the country as a whole. Moreover, many of us are oppressed by our own personal failures in Christian life and Christian ministry. We are conscious that we fall short both of the

---

1. Cf. C. E. B. Cranfield, *A Critical and Exegetical Commentary on the Epistle to the Romans* (Edinburgh, 1975), I:371.

experience of the early church and of the plain promises of
God in his Word. We are thankful indeed for what God has
done and is doing, and we do not want to denigrate his grace
by minimizing it. But we hunger and thirst for more. We long
for 'revival,' an altogether supernatural visitation of the Holy
Spirit in the church, and meanwhile for a deeper, richer, fuller
experience of the Holy Spirit in our own lives.[2]

We do not need more frightening punishments and more
withering scoldings. We need the all-sufficiency of Jesus
applied in rich measure to our deepest points of personal need.
And that is what the Holy Spirit does. He internalizes the
triumphs of Christ crucified within the depths of the human
being, so that our inclinations start changing from evil to good.
The law cannot do that. The law tells us to pump harder, but
the Holy Spirit makes springs of living water flow from
within. The law tells us to pedal faster, but the Holy Spirit
fills our sails. And that is the power of real holiness.

But Paul does not begin Romans chapter 8 with the
ministries of the Spirit. After the anguish of chapter 7, Paul
first reassures us of our bedrock confidence before God: our
union with Christ. Verse 1 declares, 'There is therefore now
no condemnation for those who are in Christ Jesus.' If God
has drawn you to himself, then he has put you 'in Christ Jesus'.
We have been '*united with him* in a death like his,' and 'we
shall certainly be *united with him* in a resurrection like his'
(Romans 6:5). Jesus used a metaphor to convey the vital
intimacy of our union with him: 'I am the vine, you are the
branches' (John 15:5). We can see how striking this reality is
from Philippians 1:1, where Paul addresses his letter 'to all
the saints *in* Christ Jesus who are *in* Philippi' (NASB). Right
now I am in Augusta, Georgia. You may be in Los Angeles

---

2. John R. W. Stott, *The Baptism and Fullness of the Holy Spirit* (Chicago, 1964), page 3.

or in Edinburgh or in Johannesburg. But far more, you and I are also in Christ Jesus.

Think of it: 'in Christ Jesus.' Could there be a simpler way to articulate our relationship with the Lord than the word *in*? But the meaning is profound. Among other things, our union with Christ means that his righteousness has been credited to us, in God's sight (Romans 3:22; 4:3, 23-24). And that is why there is 'no condemnation for those who are in Christ Jesus.'

God has done this, we did not. And it changes everything. It means that we are not holding on to Christ as much as he is holding on to us. It means that God has done something for us larger than our own change of allegiance to him. He has included us in all that the death and resurrection of Jesus are worth. So when we prove again that we are sinners, as we too often do, we may also announce to ourselves that we are also in Christ Jesus, as liable to condemnation as he is.[3]

God wants us to revel in our union with his Son. Martyn Lloyd-Jones counsels us in how to take advantage of this triumph of grace:

---

3. James Montgomery Boice, *Romans: Volume 2, The Reign of Grace* (Grand Rapids, 1992), page 795, notes that Paul refers to the believer's union with Christ ('in Christ,' 'in Christ Jesus,' 'in him' or their equivalents) no less than 164 times in his letters. He observes:

In his writings Paul illustrates the concept by three very powerful illustrations. The first is the union of the head and the body, in which he compares the members of the church to the various parts of Christ's body (cf. 1 Cor. 12:12-27; Eph. 1:22-23; Col. 1:18). The second is the union of the parts of a building, sometimes described as a temple that has the Lord Jesus Christ as its chief cornerstone (cf. 1 Cor. 3:9, 11-15; Eph. 2:20-22). The third and most powerful illustration is the union of a husband and wife in marriage. Paul ends his teaching about marriage by saying, 'This is a profound mystery – but I am talking about Christ and the church' (Eph. 5:32).

If you have got hold of this idea you will have discovered the most glorious truth you will ever know in your life. Most Christian people are miserable, most Christian people fail, and fall into sin, because they are depressed, because they allow the devil to depress them. 'Ah,' they say, 'I have sinned, so how can I make these great statements?' Have you never heard of the word 'faith'? This verse is the answer of faith to all our troubles; this is what God tells us about ourselves; and He puts it in this absolute, complete, certain manner.[4]

Should we not declare to ourselves what God so clearly declares to us here in Romans 8:1? Thirty years ago, as a college student, when I was wrestling with my own mediocrity, I wrote out the following on a piece of note-paper, which I have before me right now:

I'm so full of myself.
I'm so frustrated.
I'm so defeated.
I'm so discouraged.
I'm so sad.
BUT
Christ is SUFFICIENT.
Christ is VICTORIOUS.
Christ is SOVEREIGN.
Christ is CAPABLE.
Christ is LOVING.
AND
I'm FORGIVEN.
So PRESS ON! AND DON'T LOOK BACK!!!

---

4. D. M. Lloyd-Jones, *Romans: An Exposition of Chapters 7:1-8:4, The Law: Its Functions and Limits* (Edinburgh, 1995 reprint), page 277.

Simply put, but isn't that the foundation we all stand on? Isn't that consistent with the plain absoluteness of Paul's declaration here? What a contrast with the tortuous self-analysis of Romans 7! Only an unambiguous proclamation like this has the power to release the human conscience into freedom to live joyfully for God.

Interestingly, some manuscripts of the Greek New Testament add something to the end of the verse, to qualify it. The Authorized (or King James) Version translates these manuscripts: 'There is therefore now no condemnation to them which are in Christ Jesus, *who walk not after the flesh, but after the Spirit.*' As the Greek New Testament was hand-copied in the course of the early Christian centuries, some scribe could not allow verse 1 to stand in its unqualified simplicity. So he took the last phrase of verse 4 and repeated it here at the end of verse 1, to soften the force of the verse: 'Sure, there's no condemnation for those in Christ – as long as they're walking in the Spirit!' But this change is more than a corruption of the text. It is a corruption of the gospel. After all, when are we walking deeply enough and consistently enough in the Spirit, to escape condemnation? Paul's whole point in this verse is to speak peace into the storm of our souls, calming our inner turmoil so painfully described in chapter 7. So who may allow himself to breathe in the gospel's atmosphere of gracious acceptance? 'Those who are in Christ Jesus' – period. You may or may not be walking in the Spirit at any given moment. But there is no condemnation for you, none at all[5] – not because your behavior is so Christian but because your Savior is Christ. And this is true for you right now ('There is therefore *now*

---

5. Cf. James Denney, 'St. Paul's Epistle to the Romans,' in *The Expositor's Greek Testament*, edited by W. Robertson Nicoll (Grand Rapids, 1970 reprint), II:644: 'The οὐδέν is emphatic: condemnation is in every sense out of the question.'

. . .'). Not five years from now, when you hope to be a better Christian, but right now, as you are, Jesus Christ is your absolute Savior.

Whatever the world may say, the Bible reveals that you and I are not isolated, autonomous, completely self-determining individuals. We are involved in vast and ancient solidarities – either with Adam or with Christ (Romans 5:12-21). Our guilt is more than personal. We *inherited* guilt from our forefather Adam![6] But in God's great love for us, he has removed us from our natural identification with Adam, cancelled our Adamic guilt, and joined us supernaturally to Christ Jesus so that we inherit his righteousness.

If you are in Christ, then all that he can do for a defeated failure is now *yours*. You are not going to hell any more! This brief life is all the hell you will ever know. You will never again hear God's holy law thundering its curses against you. The atoning work of Christ on your behalf is complete, and you cannot add anything to enhance his triumph (John 19:30). So never qualify the gospel with well-meaning but unscriptural add-on phrases, the way that ancient scribe did with verse 1. Have some respect for what Jesus accomplished at his cross. Let your heart find rest in the wonder of Jesus Christ: 'God made him who knew no sin to be sin on our behalf, that we might become the righteousness of God in him' (2 Corinthians 5:21). Let it sink in: at his cross, Jesus took all our sins on himself as if they were his own, so that now God gives us the righteousness of Jesus as our own. Our holy Lord exchanged places with us sinners. He put us in his

---

6. The difficulty of this biblical teaching is reflected in the subtitle of a recent book on the subject, viz., Henri Blocher, *Original Sin: Illuminating the Riddle*, edited by D. A. Carson (Grand Rapids, 1997). On page 15, Blocher quotes Augustine, who said regarding original sin, 'Nothing is so easy to denounce, nothing is so difficult to understand.'

place of approval, he put himself in our place of condemnation, and God accepts that exchange. Your only part is to open your heart and receive the finished cross-work of Christ. When you do, you are justified before God. You are not just brought up from minus to zero, to a position of neutrality. You are declared positively righteous in God's assessment of you, as righteous as Jesus himself. And that is why you are released from condemnation and enter into peace with God (Romans 5:1).

This miracle of God's love, which the Bible calls justification, not only secures us in his favor forever. It also puts into the hand of every Christian warrior a strong weapon against moral despair in the warfare of everyday temptation. The gospel is like this. God approaches you and says, 'I have here a credit card. It is the credit card of justification. It accesses the infinite resources of the merit of Christ. If you take it, you can charge all your moral debts to this card. There is no limit on this card. It will give you a new credit rating in my data base. And you can carry this card with you at all times. Whenever you sin, you can charge it to Jesus. So I will never declare you bankrupt. How about it? Will you accept the card?' And you and I have believed God's offer and stretched out our empty hands to receive his gift. So now, when we sin, we know what to do. We take out the card and, by faith, let Jesus pay for it and put us back into 'the black' with God.

Obviously, we could abuse the credit card. We could hear God's offer and respond, 'Think of the possibilities! I can go on a spending spree of sin, with no consequences!' That, of course, is hypocrisy. The credit card is only for people of faith. And faith hungers and thirsts for righteousness (Matthew 5:6). That is the only true incentive for accepting the credit card of justification. Justification is for sinners whose hearts are longing to be rid of their sin. And for them, it really is as free and as wonderful as that credit card.

Verse one does *not* say, 'There are no sins, there are no accusations, there are no valid complaints, there are no disciplines.' A Christian is not above correction. A Christian is not always right. *But a Christian is never condemned under the judgment of God.* The gospel does not deny the enslaving grip of sin ('the law of sin *and death*,' verse 2), but the gospel does deny the damning authority of sin. When you affirm your new identity in Christ, you are not playing a pretend game. You are not covering over your problems. But you are seeing yourself and your problems in a new connection – in relation to all that Jesus is worth to you, with his blood cleansing you and his promises securing your future. In fact, your union with Christ says more about you in the sight of God than your own habits and mood swings and weaknesses (and strengths!) say about you. The way God sees it, your real moral guilt died at the cross. *So if you are in Christ, then all your sins – past, present and future – are already in your past.* They are a settled matter in the sight of God even now. You may need to make some apologies to people you have offended. You may need to confess sins and repair damage. But even as you go about doing those things, you go with the smile of God to encourage you along. You can even put your own name right here in the Bible: 'There is therefore now no condemnation for _____, who is in Christ Jesus.'

Now, if you have God's approval in Christ, can it be wrong to relish a *sense* of his approval? Do not think, 'If I want to be an earnest Christian, I can't allow myself to *enjoy* the smile of God.' Do not take yourself that seriously. Do not trust in yourself at all. Self-reproach does not bind you to godliness; confidence in Christ does. Trust him as your all-sufficient Savior. Romans 8:1 is *announcing* to you with unqualified clarity the absoluteness of your acceptance in Christ. God not only accepts you, he wants you to *know* that he accepts you, because you will never see liberating breakthroughs to new levels of personal holiness except in the reassuring atmosphere of grace.

Living under condemnation actually strengthens sin. How? Given that the demands of God's holy law are unendurable for weak sinners like us, sinning then becomes an outlet, an attractive escape, a way of easing the pressure. But here is our only remedy: 'Spiritual health never comes from belittling sin, but from a willingness to *bathe its filthy entirety in the compassion of God.*'[7] Will you bathe your filthy entirety in the compassion of God? He longs for you to. At what point will you allow yourself to let go of your self-hatred and rejoice in the all-sufficiency of Christ? Two things are certain about you today. One, your sins will run up a debt with God, more than you know. Two, God will cover for you. Why? Because the value of the crucified One has been applied to your account. And if God has actually done this, doesn't it stand to reason that he wants you to feel loved and provided for? If you cannot 'glorify and enjoy God' through Christ, how *can* you fulfill your 'chief end'?[8]

But union with our Lord not only saves us from God's wrath and restores us to his favor. It also opens up to us a new, hopeful arrangement for living: 'For the law of the Spirit of life has set me free in Christ Jesus from the law of sin and death' (verse 2). God has structured for us a new relationship with him, in which every provision for a weak sinner is already built in and it will take nothing less than eternity in heaven to prove how vast its potentialities really are.

---

7. Bryan Chapell, *In the Grip of Grace: When You Can't Hang On: The Promises of Romans 8* (Grand Rapids, 1992), page 27. Italics added.

8. Cf. Westminster Shorter Catechism, Question 1: 'What is the chief end of man?' Answer: 'Man's chief end is to glorify God and to enjoy him for ever.'

We cannot overrate the importance of Romans 8:2 for understanding authentic Christianity. What is Paul saying here? He is only restating what the Bible says many times elsewhere. Jeremiah and Ezekiel, for example, prophesied a new covenant replacing the old covenant (Jeremiah 31:31-34; Ezekiel 36:25-28). God's holy law was originally chiselled into stone plates. It rightly condemned our every violation of holiness as real moral guilt before God. But God promised a new arrangement, a new covenant. He promised to take our guilt away and inscribe his law on our very personalities. This he accomplishes by virtue of our union with Christ ('in Christ Jesus').[9]

Basic to Christianity is the contrast between legalism and spirituality. Legalism is externalized holiness, while spirituality is internalized holiness. And spirituality produces the kind of people the law had in mind all along. The 'law of sin and death', as Paul calls it here, is human virtue confined to legalism. It is trying to meet the challenge of God's holy law through our own self-mastery. Really, it only reinforces sin, concealed under a veneer of self-righteousness. But still, legalism is attractive to the human heart, because it reduces righteousness to humanly manageable dimensions. It reduces holiness to sin management, behavior modification. Lacking God's Spirit, however, it only produces death. It hollows a person out. It turns righteousness into a role play, and make-believe moral character is unsustainable. Paul confessed his own frustration in chapter 7: 'I see in my members [the way I actually live] another law at war with the law of my mind [the way I know I ought to live] and *making me captive to the law of sin* that dwells in my members. Wretched man that

---

9. Richard F. Lovelace, *Dynamics of Spiritual Life* (Downers Grove, 1979), page 74: 'Spiritual life flows out of union with Christ, not merely imitation of Christ.'

I am!' (Romans 7:23-24a). That voice is the moan of human bondage to sin! Up from the dungeon of sin – it is 'the law of sin' in 7:23 and 'the law of sin and death' in 8:2 – up out of that misery, our weary hearts cry for liberation: 'Who will deliver me from this body of death?' (Romans 7:24b). And boot-strapping ourselves up by God's law does not deliver us. It only intensifies our frustration. It binds us to our sinful patterns, even as it makes us pretend to be something we really aren't.

But God has opened up a hopeful future. He has replaced the best that *we* can do with the best that *he* can do. The 'law of the Spirit of life' has set us free from the inexorable downward pull of the 'law of sin and death'. You and I will not be sinful like this forever. The sovereign Spirit of God has taken us on as his personal project.

Romans 8:2 could not declare more clearly that true spirituality is different from our own religious intuitions. Paul gives us only two alternatives here – life in the Spirit, and death under the law. And the difference between them is marked by the verb 'set free'. There is no bondage in authentic Christianity. It is a liberation.

But isn't it interesting that Paul calls our new arrangement for living 'the *law* of the Spirit of life'? We are freed from one law, not to be lawless, but to live under another law.

The law of sin and death we all understand from bitter experience. But the *law* of the Spirit of life? Why does Paul describe deliverance – 'Who will deliver me?' (7:24) – in terms of another law? Because Spirit-filled living is God's *authoritative* replacement for law-punished living. Ironically, in God's kingdom, legalism is illegal! It violates the law of the Spirit of life. So God's liberating new order for human existence in Christ is the exuberance of the Spirit setting us free from the exactitude of the law. Spirituality replaces legality. Life transcends religiosity.

Archibald Alexander, the nineteenth-century Princeton theologian, was confronted by a man who demanded of him, 'Sir, have you *no religion*?' And Alexander replied, 'None to speak of.'[10] But this godly man had life in the Holy Spirit, according to God's authoritative decree.

Do you see how the gospel *humbles* us? For a hell-deserving sinner to be given a whole new life at the cost of the Son of God and by the power of the Holy Spirit is a joy to inspire awe. Do you see how the gospel *encourages* us? To live in a penalty-free zone in Christ and to come under the gracious sovereignty of the Holy Spirit who writes the law of God on the human heart – that is a liberation to energize fighters. And do you see how the gospel *searches* us? The most deeply probing word here in Romans 8:1-2 is the little pronoun 'me' in verse 2. Can your heart say with the hymn-writer, 'No condemnation now I dread, Jesus and all in him is *mine*'? Can you say with Paul, 'The law of the Spirit of life has set *me* free'? Does 'set free' describe what God has done in your life? Have you really come into Christ, or are you just devoutly religious? *Are you a Christian?* Seek the Lord, and do not rest until you can say for yourself, 'The law of the Spirit of life has set *me* free from the law of sin and death.'

---

10. Cited in a review of David B. Calhoun, *Princeton Seminary, Volume I, Faith and Learning, 1812-1868*, in *The Princeton Seminary Bulletin* 17 N.S. (1996): 267.

Chapter Two

Righteousness Fulfilled in Us

³ For God has done what the law, weakened by the flesh, could not do. By sending his own Son in the likeness of sinful flesh and for sin, he condemned sin in the flesh, ⁴ in order that the righteous requirement of the law might be fulfilled in us, who walk not according to the flesh but according to the Spirit.

The new life in Christ is not a superior religion. It is God's alternative to human religion. Religion may arise from various motives. At its best, religion tries to enforce morality. It draws lines and punishes trespassers. But human religion cannot change hearts. And real goodness, strong goodness, springs from the heart.

In his great love for us, God is doing what religion cannot do. He is liberating us from the failure of religion and re-creating us in the image of Jesus Christ. C. S. Lewis reminds us that 'the dullest and most uninteresting person you talk to may one day be a creature which, if you saw it now, you would be strongly tempted to worship.'[1] That is the glorious destiny of everyone united with Christ. And that is something religion could never accomplish. But God has resolved to perfect this very miracle in us. Jonathan Edwards measured the greatness of the miracle this way:

> I am bold to say that the work of God in the conversion of one soul, considered together with the source, foundation and purchase of it, and also the benefit, end and eternal issue of it, is a more glorious work of God than the creation of the whole material universe. It is the most glorious of God's works, as it above all others manifests the glory of God.[2]

Your transformation is a more glorious miracle than the creation of the universe! For a sinful human being to change, really change, from the inside out (with authentic righteousness) and not from the outside in (with imitation righteousness), is a mega-miracle. But God can do it. God intends to do it. And the first step in his project of

---

1. C. S. Lewis, 'The Weight of Glory,' in *The Weight of Glory and Other Addresses* (Grand Rapids, 1974 reprint), page 15.
2. Jonathan Edwards, 'Thoughts on the Revival,' in *The Works of Jonathan Edwards* (Edinburgh, 1979 reprint), I:379.

transformation is to raise over us the banner, 'No condemnation!' Immediately we relax, because we know that if at any point God's project is vulnerable to our own folly, we will surely bungle it. So God assures us that no condemnation hangs over our heads, for he has joined us to Jesus Christ.

In Christ, our existence is no longer confined to sin and death. But how different it is for all who are outside Christ! Broken dreams, disillusionment, emptiness – this is all they can ever expect out of life, however valiantly they may choose to believe otherwise. On every hand we see the acids of sin eating away at the human glory that God created. Look at our aging rock stars, for example, whose money cannot conceal the real-life consequences of their sinful choices. And Sin, gloating and chuckling over his slaves, surveys his dark kingdom with sadistic glee, while poor Religion stands by powerless to set anyone free. When you left religion to become a Christian, did you think you were giving anything up? In Christ we have a new status, a new identity, a new future. God has given us his life-giving Spirit. *We have been supernaturalized!*

In Romans 8:3-4 Paul explains why God's grace will triumph where religion has failed. And that reason is God himself. Do you see the Trinitarian logic of these verses? *God the Father* sent *his Son* so that his law would be fulfilled in those who walk by *the Spirit*. All-that-God-is gives all-that-God-can-give, to transform a sinner. It takes nothing less than a miracle of the Triune God to lift you out of the ditch you have fallen into and get you going in newness of life.[3] And God *has* given himself to you.

---

3. Leon Morris, 'The Theme of Romans,' in W. Ward Gasque and Ralph P. Martin, editors, *Apostolic History and the Gospel* (Exeter, 1970), pages 249-263, argues that God himself is the primary theme of Romans. 'Romans is a book about God' (page 263). After

The reason Christians do not glorify and enjoy God more is that they do not look beyond themselves. They look into themselves, finding either demoralizing failure or (far worse) an illusion of success. They live in either self-hatred or self-admiration. But either way, they are bound up within themselves, with far too little certainty and joy. But the gospel emphasizes what *God* does – God in all the fullness of his being for all the need that you have. That is encouraging.

Let's ask four questions of verses 3-4. First, what was the law powerless to do? Secondly, why was it powerless to do that? Thirdly, what has God done to replace the failure of the flesh? Fourthly, how does God's initiative transform us today?

First, Paul writes, 'For God has done what the law ... could not do.' But what was God's law powerless to do? We know the answer from chapter 7, where Paul agonized over his own inner contradictions and hypocrisies. He admired godliness. And outwardly he achieved it – according to the letter of the law, anyway (Philippians 3:6b). But he also discovered within himself coveting – envying, resenting, lusting and pouting -- the very contradiction of everything he respected. And God's law could not lift a finger to help him. The law exposed him, confronted him and even motivated him; but it could not change him. Do you know when transformation begins? When your heart hears, as only the heart can hear, the divine verdict, 'No condemnation!' The law demands your

---

the definite article (1105x), κάι (274x), ἐν (172x) and αὐτός (156x), the next most frequently used word in Romans is θεός (153x). 'Apart from prepositions, pronouns and the like, no word in Romans approaches the frequency of 'God'' (page 250). 'The word 'God' occurs in Romans more often than in any other book in the New Testament except Acts where it is found 166x. ... In Romans θεός occurs on an average once in every 46 words, in Acts once in 110. . . . No other book in the New Testament has this same concentration on the God-theme' (page 251).

condemnation. Like human Reason in Pope's 'Essay on Man,' God's law is 'a sharp accuser, but a helpless friend.'[4] Hearing its sharp accusations, our despair only reinforces our sinful ways. But grace breaks that bondage and begins transformation. Only grace melts the heart into repentance. Only grace imparts a love for the Lord. Do not fear grace. Run toward it. God's grace is the most powerful force for good in the universe.

Secondly, why is law powerless to transform us? We are talking about God's law, not some petty form of human manipulation. Why is God's law incapable of changing us? Paul says here that it was 'weakened by the flesh'. The law is not weak. It exposes us with inescapable power. But its effect for good is weakened by the flesh.

Here for the first time in Romans 8 we encounter the word *flesh.*[5] This is an important word in Paul's vocabulary. What does he mean by it? Obviously, he means something more profound than the stuff of the human body *per se*. He means *our natural moral potential*. We might equate 'the flesh' with our nastiness, our willfulness, our lusts, and so forth. And that is a valid connection to make, since 'the works of the flesh are fornication, impurity,' and so forth (Galatians 5:19-21). But there is a subtlety here we should not miss. By 'the flesh' Paul simply means what you and I naturally are, including even our religious and moral capacities. Give me three square meals a day, eight hours of sleep at night, and I can be good – for perhaps as much as five minutes at a time.

---

4. Alexander Pope, 'Essay on Man,' in *12 Poets*, edited by Glenn Legget (New York, 1958), page 77.

5. The New International Version paraphrases with 'the sinful nature'. But that interpretation would bias the English reader to link 'the flesh' with sinful behavior, when 'the flesh' is more pervasive and more clever than that. Moreover, one should not lose the contrast implicit in 'the flesh' *versus* 'the Spirit' in Romans 8.

But it is the goodness of the flesh. And it only conceals my real sinfulness within.

The flesh can appear promising and even feel virtuous. We know that, because Paul asks the Galatian Christians, 'Are you so foolish? Having begun by the Spirit, are you now being perfected by the flesh?' (Galatians 3:3, NASB). They thought they would be *better* Christians by the flesh – even better than if they were Spirit-filled! That is how convincing and intuitive and obvious the flesh is to us. But life in the flesh, however sincere, weakens godliness. Our native religiosity produces self-righteous people who refuse to face their problems. And the more earnest they are, the more Pharisaical – zealous (in their own way), but always looking for loopholes. And how can the holiness of God's law flourish in that kind of soul, however devout? The opposite of grace is not law but the flesh, including our native goodness. You may be a fleshly Playboy or a fleshly Pharisee, but it is the same flesh.

As a boy, I remember walking to school as winter thawed into spring. Pools of water from freshly melted snow beckoned to me as I made my way along Birch Lane. I just had to stop, pick up a stick and stir that water. Lo and behold, the crystal clarity of the puddle turned brown as clouds of silt and mud swirled up from the bottom of the puddle. And that is a picture of the flesh, of you and me in our natural born condition. We can look so good, so clear, so pure. But when the stick of adversity or stress or a bad mood provokes us and stirs us up, all the filth that had been lying so quietly, unseen deep within us, swirls up to reveal what we really are. When you and I do wrong, we are not nice people who happen to make a bad decision; we are evil people proving what we really are. And people like us, in the flesh, weaken the moral force of God's holy law.

Thirdly, what has God done to replace the failure of the

flesh? 'By sending his own Son in the likeness of sinful flesh and for sin, he condemned sin in the flesh.' The fatal partnership of God's holy law with our unholy flesh could not be adjusted and improved. It had to be condemned and replaced, because we sinners, limited to our own good intentions, need more than a new method for self-improvement. We need a Savior.

That is why God sent his own Son 'in the likeness of sinful flesh'. The key word here is *likeness*, suggesting a two-fold truth about Jesus. On the one hand, the eternal Son of God, equal with the Father in deity, power and glory, came down to take to himself sinless human nature. He was truly a man, like us ('likeness'). He refused to stand at a distance and fiddle with our problem with a surgical instrument held at arm's length. No, he got down here and worked among us. He got involved, because he wanted to bring redemption *from within*. He aimed at a radical cure. But on the other hand, he was not entirely like us. He did not come in sinful flesh but in the likeness of sinful flesh. The word *likeness* does not remove him from us, but the opposite; it brings him near. And yet it does not make him identical with us, either. He remained the sinless Lamb of God even as he moved among us as one of us.

And as a man, vulnerable to death, he came 'for sin', or as the NIV paraphrases, 'to be a sin offering.' In the Old Testament God's people were to sacrifice a sin offering – a bull or goat, for example (Leviticus 4:1-5:13). The animal's blood washed away the atrocity of human sin. But at his cross Jesus was the ultimate sin offering. The Lord laid on him the iniquity of us all (Isaiah 53:6). So do not think of the Old Testament sin offering as obsolete. It is not obsolete; it is brought to consummation in Jesus. The blood of the Lamb is still washing sinners clean. It is not just in the history books. The cleansing continues. It is yours right now.

That is *why* there is no condemnation for us who are in Christ. God has already condemned our sins: '[God] condemned sin in the flesh,' Paul writes. Right down here in the human nature of our representative Head, Jesus Christ, God condemned our sins at his cross. So the law cannot dictate the terms any more. Its punishments have been inflicted. Its fury is spent. The law is silenced in its condemning authority, the religion of the flesh is shamed in its pathetic weakness, and Jesus stands forth as the Lamb of God who takes away the sin of the world. God has given us One whose mission ('by sending'), whose nature ('in the likeness of sinful flesh') and whose sacrifice ('for sin') argue that he is himself all that we sinners need. Away with all miniaturized versions of Christianity, shrunk down to the smallness of human religion! Look to Jesus. And do not project onto him your own failed experiments in Christianity-mixed-with-religion. He is not your problem. You are your problem, and he is your only answer. So what are you waiting for? Break the faith barrier and embrace all that he is for all that you need.

Fourthly, how does God transform us today? By the Spirit's influence: 'in order that the righteous requirement of the law might be fulfilled in us, who walk not according to the flesh but according to the Spirit' (verse 4). God aims to make us not just forgiven people but new people. He joins sanctification to justification. He sends the Spirit to transform us, replacing religion ('walk according to the flesh') with spirituality ('walk according to the Spirit'). And because he is the Holy Spirit, true spirituality marks a child of God with real holiness radiating from a natural, winsome human personality.

But look how categorically Paul argues. He does not say, 'in order that the righteous requirement of the law might be fulfilled in us who walk according to the Spirit.' If he had put it that way, I would not have noticed that anything was

missing. But in fact he includes a denial before his affirmation:
'. . . us who walk *not* according to the flesh *but* according to
the Spirit.' Authentic Christian living *excludes* the religiosity
of the flesh. And instead – not in addition, but instead – the
Holy Spirit makes us alive to everything agreeable with the
righteous requirement of his law.

So we can see here that Paul is making a positive statement
about God's moral law. It is still in force. Our failures to
obey the law do not nullify it; our failures only make God's
power absolutely vital. 'I will put my law in their minds and
write it on their hearts,' God promised, according to the New
Covenant (Jeremiah 31:33). His law must be internalized
within us through the Holy Spirit's transforming power. He
honors God's law by setting us apart with the personal traits
that fulfill the law's moral intent (Galatians 5:16-23). We do
not become sinless in this life, but the Spirit does authenticate
our faith by drawing our hearts up to God and everything
that pleases him.

This is authentic Christianity. What generates real holiness
is not fear of punishment but fullness of heart. When you sin,
when I sin, there is always a reason. We sin because we believe
that it is simply the price we have to pay for a taste of
happiness. But sin is deceiving us. It does not deliver on its
promise. It leaves only the bitter after-taste of death. God
promises us life. The Spirit moves in our hearts to trust God
enough to fight for life and happiness and all we desire not in
sin but in the ways of God. The Spirit arouses our thirst for
Jesus, so that we come to him and drink, until rivers of living
water flow from our inmost beings (John 7:37-39). The Spirit
shows us how wide and long and high and deep is the love of
God. He helps us to know this love that surpasses knowledge,
so that we are filled with all the fullness of God (Ephesians
3:14-19). And when we live in that holy atmosphere, sin is a
lot less attractive.

Do not think, 'I have God's Spirit, but I also have problems. So, what difference does the Spirit make?' Instead think, 'I have problems, but I also have the Holy Spirit. Therefore, I have hope!' Preach the gospel to yourself every day. And on the Lord's Day, if you go to church empty and weary and defeated, with nothing to offer, you have gone to the right place. Jesus said, 'Come to me, all who labor and are heavy laden, and I will give you rest' (Matthew 11:28, RSV).

This is why the heart is vital in authentic Christianity. We must have the felt love of God in our hearts (Romans 5:5). If we do not, if we stop short of it and settle for a cerebral faith only, an intellectual faith only, we will not be able to overcome sin. We may conceal it. We may even blind ourselves to it by redefining it. But we will be powerless to rise above its seductions, because they are aimed at the heart, where only the Holy Spirit can renew us. Let the Holy Spirit prove to you that your longings can be satisfied and his law fulfilled in you. It is his professional business.

Chapter Three

The Spiritual Mentality

[5]For those who live according to the flesh set their minds on the things of the flesh, but those who live according to the Spirit set their minds on the things of the Spirit. [6]To set the mind on the flesh is death, but to set the mind on the Spirit is life and peace. [7]For the mind that is set on the flesh is hostile to God, for it does not submit to God's law; indeed, it cannot. [8]Those who are in the flesh cannot please God.

As a student at Aberdeen University years ago, my office was located almost at the top of Cromwell Tower. (I cannot say that I passed my days of research in an ivory tower. It was only granite. But granite was good enough for me.) Set into the wall down near the entrance to the Tower, so that I walked past it every day, was a plaque in memory of Henry Scougal. Scougal taught at Aberdeen in the seventeenth century and wrote the classic of spirituality, *The Life of God in the Soul of Man*. His book influenced John Wesley and George Whitefield, among many others, and remains compelling to this day.

In this remarkable book Scougal argues that the essence of Christianity is not correct opinions or godly disciplines or rapturous ecstasies. The essence of authentic Christianity is the life of God in the soul of man, a new impulse of holy vitality imparted by God himself. And that divine life is what motivates solid Christian faithfulness. But Scougal knew the tug of the world on our hearts as well. So he wisely observed, 'The love of the world and the love of God are like the scales of a balance; as the one falleth, the other doth rise.'[1]

What marks a Christian is love for God rising above love for the world. Even more basically, what marks a Christian is not sinlessness but aspiration. When God's grace opens a window into the sin-darkened prison of your soul, a shaft of pure light falls on your uplifted face. You see everything in a new way, and you can never be the same again. Before God came, you just tried to make the best of your prison, pretty much the way everyone else does. You bought your pleasures there. You built your life there. You even cultivated your religion there. But when the life of God enters your soul through the Holy Spirit, you come to realize that there is more

---

1. Henry Scougal, *The Life of God in the Soul of Man* (London, 1961 reprint), page 64. Reprinted by Christian Focus Publications, with an Introduction by J.I. Packer.

for you than anything this world can offer. Your soul opens up to a whole new world.

In Romans 8:5-8 Paul contrasts the spiritual mentality with the worldly mentality. We need to know the difference, because it is spirituality that fulfills God's law. Verses 5-8 explain something about verse 4. According to verse 4, God sent his Son into the world so that the righteous requirement of the law would be fulfilled in us who walk according to the Spirit. This is why Jesus came – to transform us into people out of whom authentic righteousness flows from the fullness of the Holy Spirit within. Verses 5-8 go on to explain what a supernaturalized human personality actually looks like and how such a person is different from a merely natural personality.

'For those who live according to the flesh set their minds on the things of the flesh, but those who live according to the Spirit set their minds on the things of the Spirit,' Paul writes in verse 5. Our English translation includes the verb *live* in this verse: 'those who *live* according to the flesh . . . .' But there is no verb *live* in Paul's Greek text. He is going deeper than lifestyles and habits and how-to's. The NASB shows us Paul's literal wording: 'For those who *are* according to the flesh' and 'those who *are* according to the Spirit.' He is describing two diametrically opposed orientations to life underlying and controlling the way we live.

At bottom, there are not a zillion different types of people in the world. We devise many ways of distinguishing people – Democrats and Republicans, Labour and Conservative, rich and poor, stylish and stodgy, and so forth. And one can mix and match from all these categories (and more) to create a composite profile for any given individual. Marketers do this effectively. But our superficial human distinctions, though helpful in some ways, say nothing about us at the most profound level of our beings. Verse 5 peels away all the surface appearances, revealing only two types of people in all the world – those who are according to the flesh, and those who are according to the Spirit. I will call the one 'sensate man' and the other 'spiritual man'.

Sensate man is the person whose whole orientation to life is centered on earthly things offering earthly pay-offs, and spiritual man is the person whose whole orientation to life is centered on spiritual things promising heavenly pay-offs. One person's heart is charmed and fascinated and rewarded by the treasures of this world, and the other person's heart is charmed and fascinated and rewarded by the treasures of a higher world.

For example, television broadcasts the values of sensate man with the most sophisticated technology ever invented. How many channels can a satellite dish pick up, most of them crowded with mindless thrills, visceral gratification and self-display? But, perhaps surprisingly, sensate man can also be religious. The sensate and the religious are compatible, because they are both earthly. The Pharisees were devoutly religious, but it was all about earthly things. They loved the social prestige of religious position (Matthew 23:5-7). They loved the financial rewards of ministry (Luke 16:14). They 'worked the system' to squeeze earthly perks out of God's law (Mark 7:1-13). Religion and spirituality are not the same thing! And real Christianity is *spirituality* – having one's mind set on the things of the Spirit.

In Romans 6:11 Paul calls it being 'alive to God.' The psalmists put it in their own way:

My soul thirsts for God, for the living God.
When can I go and meet with God? (Psalm 42:2)

O God, you are my God,
earnestly I seek you;

> my soul thirsts for you,
> my body longs for you,
> in a dry and weary land
> where there is no water. (Psalm 63:1)

> Whom have I in heaven but thee?
> And there is nothing on earth I desire besides thee.
> (Psalm 73:25)

That is the voice of spiritual man. And that great heart for
God fulfills his law without any need for nit-picky legal
inspection. That heart is biblical Christianity. That voice is
what a supernaturalized person sounds like.

When Paul says that some people have their *minds* set on
the things of the flesh and others have their *minds* set on the
things of the Spirit, he is not using the word *mind* in a merely
intellectual sense. He is talking about our mindset ('. . . *set*
their *minds* . . .'). He is talking about our whole mentality,
what we dwell upon, the tilt of our likes and dislikes, what
we respect and admire, what we want out of life, what we
aspire after. The paraphrase by J. B. Phillips is telling: 'The
carnal attitude sees no further than natural things. But the
spiritual attitude reaches out after the things of the Spirit.'[2]

Paul himself was like this. He discovered in Jesus a treasure
so rich that he took all his hard-won lifetime achievement
awards and junked them in order to have Jesus. And then he
looked at that pile of earthly prizes there in the dumpster,

---

2. John Owen defines the spiritual mentality as the mind's
'conception of spiritual things and the setting of its affections on
them as finding that relish and savour in them wherewith it is pleased
and satisfied.' Cf. 'The Grace and Duty of Being Spiritually Minded,'
in *The Works of John Owen* (Edinburgh, 1979 reprint), VII:270. He
explicitly denies that the mind set on the Spirit is 'a notional
conception of things only' (page 269).

threw his head back and laughed: 'I count everything as loss because of the surpassing worth of knowing Christ Jesus my Lord. For his sake I have suffered the loss of all things, and count them as refuse, in order that I may gain Christ' (Philippians 3:8, RSV). If you are a Christian, but bored, maybe you need to *lose* something. You cannot just add Jesus onto an already crowded life. So what do you need to off-load, so that your heart can feel the surpassing worth of knowing Christ? And do not stop off-loading until that sense of privilege in Jesus really starts to percolate. When our hearts thrill to his surpassing worth, the world loses its appeal.

So what sets a Christian apart is a whole outlook on life that prizes spiritual riches over earthly riches. Having one's mind set on what the Spirit desires is what marks a Christian – not a super-Christian, just an ordinary Christian. This is the psychology of faith. And it is this beautiful mentality that flowers into a sanctified, law-fulfilling human personality.

One wonders, then, how many real Christians are there in our churches today? Are *you* a Christian? Am *I*? Do not tell yourself, 'I became a Christian when I raised my hand at an evangelistic meeting years ago.' That may be how you became a Christian. But that is not how you know you are a Christian. You know that your faith is real if you find in yourself a mindset preoccupied with everything dear to the Holy Spirit.

We might allow for three categories of people where Paul allows for only two. We tend to think in terms of (1) non-Christians, (2) ordinary Christians and (3) 'spiritual' Christians. And too many church people settle into that second category – just ordinary Christians, not much different from decent non-Christians. But Paul sees only two categories: the mindset of the flesh (non-Christians), and the mindset of the Spirit (Christians). The sensate live for this world because they love it more than heaven, and the spiritual live for heaven because they love it more than this world.

The devil whispers to us, 'Don't go overboard with religion. You'll look weird. Sure, go ahead and have your Christianity. But don't go too far with it.' But as we can see here in Paul's reasoning, the difference is not between a little *more* Christianity and a little *less*; the difference is between life and death. Verse 6: 'To set the mind on the flesh is death, but to set the mind on the Spirit is life and peace.' That complex network of convictions and desires and ambitions that makes you you, that shapes your personality and orders your priorities, is either God-neglecting or God-enjoying. And Paul's point here in verse 6 is that your basic orientation in life is either killing you or energizing you. Fixing ourselves on the rewards of this life dooms us to frustration and bitterness and emptiness. But when we turn away from the world and open our hearts wide to God and all that he offers us in Christ, we discover life and peace.

Let's understand what Paul is doing here. He is not exhorting us to become more spiritually minded, though that is surely implied. But primarily, Paul is pointing out that Christians *are* spiritually minded. What identifies a real Christian is a spiritual mindset, so that the believer is ready to suffer earthly loss out of desire for the surpassing worth of knowing Jesus. If you are a Christian, the Holy Spirit is nurturing that attitude in you. And he is actively working against the earthly-mindedness still left in you – and in me.

How could he do otherwise? Verse 7: 'For the mind that is set on the flesh is hostile to God, for it does not submit to God's law; indeed, it cannot.' Without the Holy Spirit, our prejudices resist God in mistaken self-protection. This is how sin gets such a grip on us. Until the Holy Spirit breaks down the barriers of our prejudices, the mind of the flesh hates God and resents the claims of his law. The flesh may not be consciously 'hostile to God'. The flesh may love God, in its way. But the flesh loves God on its own terms, not on God's terms. The flesh never says to God, 'Not my will, but thine, be done' (Luke 22:42, RSV). Being good can be a way of being bad, if being good is a way of protecting one's little earthly kingdom from God. And then one is left exposed to the overwhelming power of one's own natural moral weakness and corruption.

Our only salvation from ourselves is the real salvation God gives in Christ. He gives such a powerful internal witness to Jesus Christ that our hearts are lifted to a new sense of his glory. God performs a miracle within us from which we can never retreat. What you and I most urgently need, therefore, is not somehow to crank ourselves up to the next level of Christian commitment – 'If only I were more committed!' The work of God has its own power. What we most urgently need is to seek the Lord for this spiritual mentality, this outlook that esteems Christ above all. What we need is not stronger will-power, but a deep persuasion that Jesus Christ is worth anything. 'For you know the grace of our Lord Jesus Christ, that though he was rich, yet for your sake he became poor, so that by his poverty you might become rich' (2 Corinthians 8:9, RSV). Who could hope for more than a Savior like that?

Too many professing Christians think that God's grace legitimates graded levels of commitment. His grace certainly does allow for failure, struggle and growth. But we do not understand God's grace if we are asking questions like, 'What's the minimum I have to do to stay at my level of commitment? How can I maintain?' The spiritual mind does not think that way. Authentic Christianity is not increasing levels of commitment grudgingly given to God; it is surrender to Jesus out of a sense of privilege in having him.

So do not measure your own Christian growth in terms of levels of commitment and sacrifice. That can look good, but it can also allow unspiritual values to dominate your soul. I give God only as much as I want, according to my level of commitment. I may give a lot, in my view. But underneath it all can lurk a hostility toward God that refuses to trust his goodness and desire his worth so much that I lose all to gain Christ. Romans 8:6 is telling us that there is no sacrifice in the spiritual mentality, but only life and peace.

David Livingstone, the pioneer missionary to Africa, understood this. He explained it to the students of Cambridge University:

> For my own part, I have never ceased to rejoice that God has appointed me to such an office. People talk of the sacrifice I have made in spending so much of my life in Africa. . . . Is that a sacrifice which brings its own blest reward in healthful activity, the consciousness of doing good, peace of mind, and a bright hope of a glorious destiny hereafter? Away with the word in such a view, and with such a thought! It is emphatically no sacrifice. Say rather it is a privilege. Anxiety, sickness, suffering or danger, now and then, with a foregoing of the common conveniences and charities of this life, may make us pause and cause the spirit to waver and the soul to sink; but let this only be for a moment. All these are nothing when compared with the glory which shall be revealed in and for us. I never made a sacrifice.[3]

Sensate man can never say that. All he sees in Christianity is loss and confinement and death. But Livingstone was a spiritual man. He was no hero in the usual sense, giving up everything he loved. No, he discovered everything he loved in surrender to Christ. He did not feel sorry for himself. He felt rich. 'To set the mind on the Spirit is life and peace.'

So Paul concludes in verse 8, 'Those who are in the flesh cannot please God.' To be 'in the flesh' is to be immersed in and controlled by sensate values. This mentality never chooses

---

3. Cf. John Piper, *Desiring God* (Sisters, Oregon, 1996), page 204.

God, never makes him its supreme delight and opposes every claim he makes. This outlook is asking the wrong questions, judging by the wrong criteria, and hoping for the wrong pay-offs. There is no hope for the mentality of the flesh. It cannot be improved. It must be replaced, because it offends God.

Jonathan Edwards knew how to nurture and encourage the spiritual mentality. In a sermon from the Song of Solomon 5:1 ('Eat, O friends, and drink; drink deeply, O lovers!'), Edwards proposed that 'persons need not and ought not to set any bounds to their spiritual and gracious appetites.' He argued that

> as the covetous man desires earthly riches, so the regenerated person desires spiritual riches. He esteems grace in his soul as the best riches. He looks upon wisdom as better than gold and silver, and he is ambitious of the honor which is of God to be a child of God and an heir of glory. And as the sensualist eagerly pursues sensual delights, he longs for those pleasures that are spiritual. . . . Men may be as covetous as they please (if I may so speak) after spiritual riches and as eager as they please to heap up treasure in heaven, or as ambitious as they please of spiritual and eternal honor and glory, and as voluptuous as they please with respect to spiritual pleasure. . . . Neither ought persons to rest in any past or present degree of gracious appetite or enjoyment of the objects of it but to their utmost to be increasing the same, to be endeavoring by all possible ways to influence their desires and to obtain more spiritual pleasures.[4]

How good of God, that he would mark the way of holiness along the path of the deepest, truest pleasure! Let's spit the worldly poisons out of our mouths and taste the pure goodness of the Lord, for the spiritual mentality is the mark of God's true people.

---

4. I thank Prof. Don Westblade of Hillsdale College for this selection of Edwards, copied from a manuscript in the Yale collection.

Chapter Four

Indwelt by the Spirit

[9]You, however, are not in the flesh but in the Spirit, if in fact the Spirit of God dwells in you. Anyone who does not have the Spirit of Christ does not belong to him. [10]But if Christ is in you, although the body is dead because of sin, the Spirit is life because of righteousness. [11]If the Spirit of him who raised Jesus from the dead dwells in you, he who raised Christ Jesus from the dead will also give life to your mortal bodies through his Spirit who dwells in you.

One of the best-known poems of modern times is T. S. Eliot's 'The Hollow Men,' which begins with these lines:

We are the hollow men
We are the stuffed men
Leaning together
Headpiece filled with straw.

Then Eliot describes modern life as 'Shape without form, shade without color, Paralyzed force, gesture without motion.'[1] He really understands the frustrating contradictions pervasive in this world we have created.

God created a rich world to be enjoyed by fulfilled people, but human sin has emptied out the fullness God intended. That is why people are hollow, even as they stuff themselves with false meanings and disgusting pleasures. They do not know who they are, because they do not know the One who made them. They are empty and restless, because they are not filled with the Holy Spirit.

In his great compassion, God is not wiping the earth clean of the present human race. He is re-creating a new human race out of the wreckage that we are. God is sending out his Spirit to indwell empty people, to fill them and energize them and inspire them with new dignity. These people are called Christians. And Christians can be and should be the most authentic, convincing, natural human beings. They are *not* 'the hollow men'. They are God-filled, they are super-naturalized, and all the more human for it.

In Romans 8:9-11 Paul explains how profound and how comprehensive God's work of restoration really is. God's grace is profound, in that it touches us down at the deepest level of our being. And God's grace is comprehensive, in

---

1. T. S. Eliot, 'The Hollow Men,' in *12 Poets*, edited by Glenn Legget (Chicago, 1958), page 284.

that it spreads out to renew the whole of what we are, including our very bodies. And this infusion of renewing grace is unleashed into our existence through the Holy Spirit. God himself comes down to live within us personally, deeply, vitally.

Authentic Christianity is the life of God in the soul of man. It is the Holy Spirit dwelling within the human being. It is sheer miracle from beginning to end. Christian discipleship certainly does marshal our energies and motivate our efforts and focus our desires with an intensity we have never known before. But still, the Christian life is primarily something to be received from on high, not offered from below. Christian living is fundamentally *response* to God's in-breaking miracle. And that is why the most meaningful posture for the Christian is an open heart.

In Romans 8:1-8, Paul speaks as our teacher. He speaks principially, writing mostly in the third person, about 'those who live according to the flesh' and 'those who live according to the Spirit,' as in verse 5, for example. But here in verse 9 he addresses the Roman Christians themselves. He speaks personally. He speaks to us. The word 'you' at the beginning of verse 9 is emphatic: '*You*, however, are not in the flesh but in the Spirit.' All that Paul has said about the ministry of the Holy Spirit in verses 1-8 is *yours*. You can personalize the gospel for yourself. You can say, 'The Holy Spirit not only lives in Christians, he lives in *this* Christian.'

Paul's purpose in Romans 8 is to encourage us. He is arguing that God's grace outperforms our legalism by providing everything we need all the way to heaven, and nothing will ever separate us from God's love. Paul wants to assure us. But the word *if* here in verse 9 prompts us to ask whether God's Spirit really does live within us. Jesus said that many will come to that Final Day expecting to be received, but they will be shocked when he turns them away

(Matthew 7:21-23). So we want to be sure now that we really do belong to God. And there is no greater test of our authenticity than the marks of the indwelling Holy Spirit. If you can discern his presence in your life, there is no greater thrill than realizing, 'God Almighty in heaven is so committed to me that he has sent his very Spirit to live within me. What a privilege! What a mystery!'

Does the Holy Spirit live within you? People indwelt by the Holy Spirit still have problems, they still sin, they still make mistakes and have to offer apologies. They still suffer and weep and get sick and die, like everyone else. But if God has given you his Spirit, you find within yourself a deepening spiritual mentality (verse 6). You find that your former hostility toward God (verse 7) is melting into tenderness toward God. Once you were defensive, now you are surrendered. Once you thought God would ruin your life, now you know that God is your only happiness. You are now 'alive to God' (Romans 6:11). You still struggle. You still waver. You still sin. But God is marking you as his own.

When Paul says, in verse 9, that we are 'not in the flesh but in the Spirit,' he means that we are no longer imprisoned within our own narrow potential but are now owned by and cared for and enveloped within the all-providing, all-forgiving, all-restoring love of God. Our ultimate destiny is now determined by the transforming power of the Spirit, not by the self-defeating failures of the flesh.

Our whole existence used to be limited to the flesh – what we could achieve out of our own native moral capacities. All we had was our own good intentions. That is life in the flesh. It may be religious. It may be upright. It may be outwardly Christian. But it is rotten within, and it cannot last.

When my family and I lived in Oregon in the late 1980s, one of the trees in our back yard began to lean out over our neighbor's house. So we had to cut it down. Now and then we had a snowfall, and we did not want a nasty surprise in the middle of some January night. But when my neighbor and I cut that tree down, we discovered why it was beginning to tilt. It had rotted inside. It looked healthy on the outside, but it was hollowing out with rot. And a heavy snowfall would have brought it crashing down onto his roof. You and I are like that in our natural selves, in the flesh. We can look good. But the tilt of our lives reveals rottenness and emptiness within. And a sudden pressure or stress or temptation can bring us crashing down. God has the right to cut us down, but in his great love, he is filling us instead. That is the work of his indwelling Holy Spirit. He is renewing us from the inside out. We are not hollow any more.

What is more, this is true not just of '*good* Christians', as some might say, but of *all* Christians – every single Christian without exception. That is why Paul adds, 'if in fact the Spirit of God dwells in you. Anyone who does not have the Spirit of Christ does not belong to him.' Christians without the Holy Spirit do not exist, and all who do have the Spirit are Christians and stand to inherit all the renewal that God can impart to a rotted sinner.

Isn't it interesting how Paul heaps relationship upon relationship in these verses? He says that we are in the Spirit, if the Spirit dwells in us. He implies that, if we have the Spirit of Christ, we belong to Christ. If we belong to Christ, he is in us. But Paul's elaborate style is not rhetorical excess. He is describing the richly relational dynamic of authentic Christianity. The Holy Spirit conveys to us the nearness of Christ himself, personally and vividly. In Ephesians 3:17 Paul prays that Christ would dwell in our hearts through faith. In John 14:23 Jesus said that he and the Father would come to us and make their home with us. How does this happen? The Holy Spirit manifests the presence of God to us. When someone becomes a Christian, he does not simply change his beliefs, important as that is; a whole new relationship with God opens up. A Christian is lifted out of the isolation of the flesh into personal intimacy with the Triune God.

And it shows. The coming of the Spirit to indwell us is like taking a dropper filled with blue ink, squeezing it and letting one drop of that blue ink fall onto a blotter. The ink spreads out in all directions. If the Holy Spirit were blue, a tinge of blue would appear pervasively in our personalities. And wherever we are most clearly blue, there we are also the most alive.

Verse 10 takes our thought in that direction: 'But if Christ is in you, although the body is dead because of sin, the Spirit is life because of righteousness.' The key words here are *dead* and *life*. Your body is dead. So is mine. Yes, our hearts are still beating, but every heartbeat is one less, because of the deadening drag of sin. It began in the Garden of Eden. God said to sinful Adam, 'Dust you are, and to dust you will return' (Genesis 3:19). This is the reason we are vulnerable to pain, corruption, weakness and death. This is the reason Paul wrote of 'our vile body' (Philippians 3:21, AV). Our vitality is being eroded by the acids of death even now, and we cannot evade death's humiliating victory over us for long. Therefore, real life is not to be found in the body but in the Spirit. 'The Spirit is life,' Paul says.

The world tells us, 'If you're not in shape, if you're not thin, if you're not beautiful, if you're not sexually active, if you're not young, you're not *alive*.' But is that true? If it were true, then all the fit, thin, beautiful, sexually active young people in this world would be on Cloud Nine. But they are not. Why? Because life does not flow into our experience through the body but through the Spirit. It is the spiritual, not the physical, that gives us hope and fullness and joy. The body is not to be despised. God made our bodies. He must like them. But the fact is, sin is killing us all. And God imparts true life in our hearts, not in our veins. So do not be fooled by the world. Be filled with the Spirit. That is where life is.

The life God gives he gives 'because of righteousness', that is, because of Christ's righteousness. So the life that is truly life is already paid for in advance, in full, at his cross. He gives us true, rich and abundant life at his own expense and freely. Jesus said, 'I came that they may have life, and have it abundantly. I am the good shepherd. The good shepherd lays down his life for the sheep' (John 10:10-11, RSV). He invites us, 'Come, all you who are thirsty, come to the waters; and you who have no money, come, buy and eat! Come, buy wine and milk without money and without cost' (Isaiah 55:1, NIV). How can we buy what is not for sale? It is all of his grace.

Our fullness of life right now is only the beginning of the life we are going to experience. Verse 11: 'If the Spirit of him who raised Jesus from the dead dwells in you, he who raised Christ Jesus from the dead will also give life to your mortal bodies through his Spirit who dwells in you.' He not only reinvigorates our spirits now, he will raise our bodies too. The Spirit of God is the ultimate life-giver. He must have an infinite store of vitality within himself to fill us all now and forever, as the life he imparts spreads out to restore all that sin has ruined. There is not one ounce of you that will end up in the trashbin of the universe – except your sins, which you want to leave behind anyway. All that God has made in making you he will rejuvenate, including your body, the humblest part of you. And he will do this through the Holy Spirit, who is indwelling you even now.

It is refreshing to stand back and think how triumphant we really are through our Lord. An elder in our church specializes in oncology. In his office he has a plaque on the wall entitled 'What Cancer Cannot Do':

Cancer is so limited –
It cannot cripple love,
It cannot shatter hope,
It cannot corrode faith,
It cannot destroy peace,
It cannot kill friendship,
It cannot suppress memories,
It cannot silence courage,
It cannot invade the soul,
It cannot steal eternal life,
It cannot conquer the Spirit.

Poor, defeated Cancer, we mock you!

Of course, the Bible is not saying that God will make you eighteen again forever. Initially, that might seem attractive. But God is saying more, because when you were eighteen your youthful body was dead even then. God will raise our bodies, which even now are 'dead' (verse 10) and 'mortal' (verse 11), and he will 'give life' to our bodies at the resurrection of the just. God is promising that you are going to be *better* than when you were at your best – better by far. You have never experienced yet what you are going to be. You and I have never experienced *real* life. We have seen it, because whatever God did in raising Jesus on that first Easter Sunday he will do for us too. We will become invulnerable to death and disease and pain and aging. No more medications, no more walkers, no more arthritis, no more cancer or headaches or hormone therapy or MS or sexually transmitted diseases. No need for sleep. No sinful urges raging within. No possibility of injury. Instead, full energy, full capacities, full intensity, full control, full alertness, acute sensitivity to everything worthy in an atmosphere of unmixed, holy joy forever and ever. That is the triumph of God's Spirit in all of God's children!

Everything that this sad life steals from us, whether through drugs or war or a drunk driver or genetic disorder or disease or just plain old age – God will restore it all through the Holy Spirit, who already lives within us. Therefore, if we have the Spirit, the real crisis is past. The real crisis is not out in the future at our moment of death. Death will be a release, because the real crisis was 2000 years ago on a cross near Jerusalem where Jesus won our righteousness for us. So now, 'because of [Christ's] righteousness,' God freely and gladly sends to us his Spirit, the Lord and Giver of life, to live within us. And the Spirit is not going anywhere until he has completed his restoring miracle on that great and final Day.

What you and I are right now is hardly the consummation of our existence. It is the merest beginning. Consider the goodness and power of God. How weak we think he is! How mean we think he is! How prudish we think he is! How uncertain we feel our happiness to be! Let's listen again to the gospel and drink in with thankful joy the promises of God. Nothing is more certain than this: God will keep his good word to you, for all that it is worth, for he has given you the pledge of his Holy Spirit.

Chapter Five

Cut It Away!

[12] So then, brothers, we are debtors, not to the flesh, to live according to the flesh. [13] For if you live according to the flesh you will die, but if by the Spirit you put to death the deeds of the body, you will live. [14] For all who are led by the Spirit of God are sons of God.

Jackson Browne sings a song entitled, 'Cut It Away.' I am moved by its intensity and anguish. The lyrics, in part, go like this:

Cut it away, somebody cut away this desperate heart
Cut it away, and help me find my way back to the start

Cut it away, I want to cut away this thing inside
Cut it away, this thing that hid from you and schemed and lied

Cut it away, somebody cut away this desperate heart
Cut it away, before it tears my whole life apart.

Whether or not Jackson Browne is a Christian, he understands the radical surgery each of us needs. It is foolish just to add more to our lives. We need to cut some things away. We have some hard decisions to make. We have some courageous follow-through to undertake. But whatever this may mean for you or me, there is no denying it: Cutting away is a part of the Christian life.

In Romans 8:1-11 Paul spreads before us our resources in the Spirit-energized life. We still struggle and we still sin, because sin lives within us (Romans 7:17, 20). But now the Holy Spirit also dwells within us (8:9-11). We have been supernaturalized. *So now God calls us to demonstrate it.* How? How does a Spirit-indwelt person respond to what God has done? Paul answers that question in Romans 8:12-14.

'So then, brothers, we are debtors, not to the flesh, to live according to the flesh' (verse 12). Now isn't that a strange thing to say? Have you ever considered seriously that you had an obligation to the flesh? An obligation to God, yes. But to the flesh? Why does Paul argue for something we would agree with anyway?

Paul is thinking back to all of verses 1-11, and especially to verses 10-11. He is saying something like this: 'I look at all God has done for the people described in verses 1-11 and

I have to say, those people are not a bunch of losers! They have been empowered by God to live for God! Now, look at your own life, with all the newness God has given you. Your life is really going somewhere. God has removed all the condemnation you deserve and put it on Christ crucified. He has liberated you from the vicious cycle of sin and death. He has put you under a new arrangement of Spirit and life. He will fulfill his law in you by the Spirit. He is giving you a new, spiritual mentality, enriching you with life and peace. Christ himself has come to live within you by his Spirit, bringing life to your spirit. And he promises to raise up your mortal body on that final Day. So look at your life. Think back to your sweetest moments with the Lord thus far. Look at what you have going for you now. Relish by faith what God has promised you in the future. Now think about it. Where does your happiness come from? From the flesh, or from the Spirit? There are only two sources out of which you can live. There are only two sources to which you can look for what you hope to gain. There are only two sources you have to thank for it all. You are a debtor to one or the other. You explain your life and your joys *somehow*. So, to what do you owe everything you cherish?'

If your heart is one with Paul's, you will say with him, 'I don't owe the flesh *anything*. The flesh has been the cause of my bitterest miseries. I've served it too long, and what a price I've paid! Everything I have that's encouraging, God has given me through his Spirit. I owe him everything. I am a debtor to God. He has given me, even me, his very best.' That is what Paul wants us to feel – a sense of indebtedness to God, drawing our hearts out gratefully to him.

Or think of verse 12 this way. A certain girl has a boyfriend who peddles dope, he is abusive to her, he lies to her, he has caused her untold heartache. She owes him nothing. Good riddance! Another young man takes an interest in her. He loves her. He enriches her life immeasurably. Everything he brings into her life is worthy and joyful. She has a future with a man like that. So she looks at her life. Her old boyfriend thinks only of himself. Her new boyfriend is giving her a life worth living. All her happiness she owes to that man. And we are like that girl. We are debtors not to the flesh, to flirt with the flesh and get entangled in the same old wretchedness. 'We are debtors, but not to the flesh.'

But do you see what is missing in verse 12? After all that Paul has said in Romans 8 about the flesh *versus* the Spirit, his thought here seems incomplete. What we expect him to say is this: 'So then, brothers, we are debtors, not to the flesh, to live according to the flesh, *but to the Spirit, to live according to the Spirit.*' Isn't that what Paul's argument thus far leads us to expect? In fact, the very next verse resumes the explicit contrast between the flesh and the Spirit. Paul expects us to fill out the logical symmetry of his thought. We are not debtors to the flesh, but we are debtors to the Spirit. We owe him thanks for everything good in our lives, and we owe the flesh nothing.

Insisting on this point is helpful, because the flesh continues to make demands of us: 'If I don't get my way in this situation, I'll walk out!' 'If I never possess that longed-for thing, I can't be happy.' 'If I don't get an apology from that person who hurt me, I'll explode!' Our sinful psychology feels demands with keen sensitivity, but not debts. Our natural turn of mind diminishes our sense of gratitude and humility and inflates our sense of entitlement. We even have a duty-to-self ethic in our world today: 'I owe it to myself to follow my dream, to grow as a person – even if it costs me my marriage.' The flesh, with its expectations and requirements, demands our cooperation and threatens us with misery if we do not comply. But to meet the demands of that idol, we have to turn our backs on the goodness of God so generously poured out into our lives through his Spirit.

The flesh is asking all the wrong questions, like, 'If I commit sin X, can I still go to heaven? How can I cut corners and still keep my Christian credentials? Do I have to obey the Bible across the whole of my life?' This is the mentality of the flesh (verse 5). It reveals hostility toward God (verse 7), as if living for God were a bad deal in life. That is the way we used to feel, before we became Christians. And Paul's point here is, Where did that get us? Nowhere. But everything the Spirit brings is precious beyond calculation. 'So then, brothers, we are debtors, not to the flesh, to live according to the flesh, but to the Spirit, to live according to the Spirit.'

In the book of Proverbs the sage urges upon us this bit of homely wisdom:

> Do not withhold good from those to whom it is due,
> when it is in your power to do it.
> Do not say to your neighbor, 'Go, and come again,
> tomorrow I will give it' – when you have it with you.
>   (Proverbs 3:27-28, RSV)

God, our eternal neighbor, approaches us as we read Romans 8:12 and reminds us of the debt we owe him. We may not respond by saying, 'No, Lord. Come back later. I'll be ready then.' We cannot say that, because right now we have all the resources of Romans 8:1-11.[1] We have the Holy Spirit indwelling us right now. So when we open our wallets to pay our debt, we find them *full* of spiritual resources. God has lavished upon us 'everything we need for life and godliness' (2 Peter 1:3, NIV). Whenever our Lord confronts us, as he often does, our part is to say, 'Yes, Lord. With your help, I'll take this new step. I will not put you off. I want to draw strength from every encouragement you've given and every

---

1. Cf. H. C. G. Moule, *The Epistle to the Romans* (London, 1893), pages 219-220.

promise you've made. Let's go for it!' And when our Lord approaches us, we see not a frown on his face but glad expectations and readiness to help. He only claims what he himself has immeasurably given. Let's always be ready to give our Lord whatever he wants, because we owe him everything. So the next time he asks something of you, remember Romans 8:1-11. Who else could give you all *that*?

What is God asking of you today? What courageous new step does he want you to take in your pilgrimage? It is true that we pay a price to follow Christ. But isn't it also true that we pay a far higher price *not* to follow Christ? When we give in to our vulgar impulses and our mere likes and dislikes, when we accommodate the demands of the flesh, what do we get out of it but emptiness and regret and lost opportunities? We owe the flesh nothing. We owe the Lord everything.

Verse 13 confronts us with its stark absoluteness: 'For if you live according to the flesh you will die, but if by the Spirit you put to death the deeds of the body, you will live.' In other words, if we go by merely human standards to guide us and merely human resources to help us, we will die. Ambition, comfort, ego, self – the fleshly agenda for life – it is dead and deadening! And the only alternative to gratification of the flesh is battle by the Spirit: 'putting to death the deeds of the body.' Notice again that Paul's reasoning allows not for three categories (non-Christians, carnal Christians, and super-Christians) but only two: non-Christians and Christians. Non-Christians live according to the flesh and they die. Christians put to death the sinful deeds of the body by the power of the Spirit and they live. Stark absoluteness. It is one or the other for every one of us – either surrendering to the flesh and dying, or fighting by the Spirit and living.

Verse 13 is one of the most important verses in the Bible for living the Christian life. 'Putting to death the deeds of the body' has traditionally been called mortification, from the Latin verb *mortificare*, to kill, destroy, reduce to weakness.[2] The Authorized Version even translates verse 13, 'But if ye through the Spirit do *mortify* the deeds of the body . . . .' But what is this discipline of mortification? It is declaring war on the old life and fighting for a new life.

In 1993 Donald Wyman was clearing timber in a remote Pennsylvania forest. Tragically, a tree fell on him, pinning his left leg. For an hour he screamed for help, but there was no one to rescue him. Realizing that he would die there, Mr. Wyman tied off his leg with a tourniquet from a leather boot lace, took out his pocket knife, and cut off his leg about six inches below the knee. He then crawled back to his truck, drove to get help – and lived to tell the tale.

If you have to choose between living with one leg and dying with both legs – if you *have* to choose – is there any choice? Isn't living better than dying? What gave Mr. Wyman the courage to cut off his own leg was the realization that he could not keep it and live. It was either his leg or his life.

One reason we Christians are too soft on our sins is that we think we do have a choice. We think we can coddle our darling sins, rather than cut them away, and it will not make that much difference. But Jesus taught us otherwise. He said, 'If your eye causes you to sin, pluck it out. It is better for you to enter the kingdom of God with one eye than to have two eyes and be thrown into hell, where "their worm does not die, and the fire is not quenched" ' (Mark 9:47-48, NIV).

Or think of a rebellious college freshman, out on his own for the first time in his life. He turns his back on his past. He repudiates his upbringing. He sets himself firmly against it with a vengeance. He determines to shape a new life, a new

---

2. To explore further the meaning of mortification, see John Owen's essay on the Holy Spirit, in *The Works of John Owen* (Edinburgh, 1965), III:538-565.

identity, new values. He throws himself into becoming a completely different person. He cuts his old self away and a new self emerges. Mortification is like that.

God is calling you and me to mortify our old lives and pursue a new life in the Spirit. What would we become, if we threw ourselves into developing a new life in Christ with the same enthusiasm shown by a college freshman intent on a new life? What would happen to our churches? Do we owe less to our Lord than that freshman gives to his new allegiance? When was the last time you put something inside yourself to death? When was the last time you got tough on yourself? When was the last time you deliberately placed yourself under the judgment of the Word of God? Or are you just waiting for that somehow to happen? Verse 13 is a call to action. What is there in your life right now that needs to *die*, so that something new can *live*?

Mortification will mark us as Christians. The modern world makes huge allowances for sinful behavior. Our society's tolerance levels are off the charts. But life in the Spirit means killing our sinful impulses. The flesh cannot be refined into holiness. It needs to die.

Our world tells us that we have to let everything out, that suppressing our feelings is dishonest and even harmful. But the Bible isn't calling us to suppress our sinful urges. It's calling us to kill them. And God is saying this will do us good. If that hang-up inside you that holds you back – if it *dies*, you don't have to suppress it any longer. And you move on, a new person. This is the miracle of the Holy Spirit deep within us.

But we must act. The harsh, impatient word, the wandering, lustful eye, the greedy, grasping hand – Jesus said, 'And if your right hand causes you to sin, cut it off and throw it away' (Matthew 5:30, NIV). He was exaggerating for dramatic effect, but his point is clear. We cannot be Christians without Spirit-empowered initiative. Maybe every one of us has some

overdue action to take. The way forward for you and me –
'putting to death the deeds of the body' – is a rugged, take-
no-prisoners determination to stop pandering to the flesh and
start afresh, no matter what the personal cost. It takes courage.
But our incentive is the promise of life: 'You will live.' And
our Helper is the mighty Holy Spirit of God: 'by the Spirit.'

Mortification is not self-punishment. Mortification is not
starving yourself to lower your physical energy. Mortification is not joyless self-absorption and religious tyranny.
Mortification is not a method for living a holy life. It is not a
method; it is a mentality. It is faith at work. It is a determination to *stop dying* and *start living* in the fullness of the Holy
Spirit. It is hungering and thirsting for righteousness so much
that we act boldly to lay hold of it, looking to the Lord moment by moment for his strength.

What does verse 13 tell us about *how* we mortify our sins?
One, mortification is *relentless*. The present tense of the verb
translated 'put to death' implies on-going action. Your desire
to be made new overrules your desire to stay as you are, and
your new spiritual mentality (verse 5) sets the course of your
life all the way to heaven.

Two, mortification is *'by the Spirit'* – not by legalism.
The gospel does include conditions: 'If . . . you put to death
the deeds of the body, you will live.' But unlike legalism, the
gospel builds encouragement and power into the condition:
'If *by the Spirit* . . . .' The Holy Spirit is the one who transforms
sin-tolerating people into sin-killing people. These people
are Christians. But we have our own part in this. We are the
subject of the verb 'put to death.' Without the Spirit, we
cannot; without us, the Spirit will not.[3] The Spirit works

----

3. Cf. Stephen Charnock, 'A Discourse on Mortification,' in *The
Works of Stephen Charnock* (Edinburgh, 1997 reprint), V:214-215. I
thank Mr. Reddit Andrews for drawing my attention to Charnock at
this point.

through our faith, when we stop perceiving God with dread and start perceiving him with such eagerness that we jettison everything from our lives that clouds our view of God and welcome into our lives everything that clears our view of God. Desiring God opens our hearts to the sin-destroying ministry of the Spirit.

Three, mortification is *aimed at life*, not at mere correctness ('. . . you will *live*'). A legalist wants always to be in the right, because being in the right feels superior. A Christian wants always to be in Christ, because being in Christ lays hold of *life*. Isn't it paradoxical that killing our darling sins is the point at which we break through to life? Life comes not through the correctness of one's opinions. Life comes through death.

Four, mortification is *courageous*. The very language Paul uses – 'put to death' – implies the boldness of living in communion with the Spirit. You and I have some decisions to make every day. If you are in Christ, do not tell yourself you are a paralyzed loser: 'There's nothing I can do, I'm so sinful.' That is true, in a way, of course. But it is not the whole truth, by a long shot. The Bible also says, 'From the fullness of his grace we have all received one blessing after another' (John 1:16, NIV). The Bible says, 'God is at work in you, both to will and to work for his good pleasure' (Philippians 2:13, RSV). He has given us so much. Now he says to us, 'Be on your guard; stand firm in the faith; be men of courage; be strong' (I Corinthians 16:13, NIV).

What is God saying to you at this point in your discipleship? What have you tolerated in your life that you must today get rid of? Where have you left your flank unguarded and exposed to temptation? Jesus said, 'Watch out! Don't let me find you living in careless ease and drunkenness, and filled with the worries of this life' (Luke 21:34, NLT). Careless ease – is it even possible for modern

Christians to stay out of that trap? Drunkenness – along with over-eating and workoholism and other drugs. The worries of this life – fretting over making a big impression and the stock market and politics and so forth. Jesus said, 'Don't let me find you living this way.' Christians are people who live in the atmosphere of grace – not in careless ease and drunkenness and the worries of this life – by the power of the Spirit. Christians are a new race of mankind being created by the Spirit of God. They are normal people being led along an unmistakably new path in life: 'For all who are led by the Spirit of God are sons of God' (verse 14). Being a child of God makes an unmistakable difference, as God leads us through mortification into ever richer life. Will you open your heart to his Spirit precisely where you have been filling your emptiness with some pet substitute for God? Cut it away and let it die. Let new life be born at that very place in your soul.

Chapter Six

Assurance

[14]For all who are led by the Spirit of God are sons of God. [15]For you did not receive the spirit of slavery to fall back into fear, but you have received the Spirit of adoption as sons, by whom we cry, 'Abba! Father!' [16]The Spirit himself bears witness with our spirit that we are children of God.

The Heidelberg Catechism was written by Zacharias Ursinus (1534-1583) and Caspar Olevianus (1536-1587). Ursinus once said that he would not take a thousand worlds for the blessed assurance of being owned by Jesus Christ. And when Olevianus lay dying, a friend asked him if he was certain of his salvation. In reply, his last, dying word was 'Certissimus!' 'Most certain!'[1] This explains the spiritual depth out of which the Heidelberg Catechism makes its first, triumphant affirmation:

Question: What is your only comfort in life and in death?

Answer: That I am not my own, but belong – body and soul, in life and in death – to my faithful Savior Jesus Christ. He has fully paid for all my sins with his precious blood and has set me free from the tyranny of the devil. He also watches over me in such a way that not a hair can fall from my head without the will of my Father in heaven; in fact, all things must work together for my salvation. Because I belong to him, Christ, by his Holy Spirit, assures me of eternal life and makes me whole-heartedly willing and ready from now on to live for him.[2]

In Romans 8 Paul helps us relocate our faith from the dim twilight of man-centered hesitation to the brilliant noonday of God-centered assurance, so that we become whole-heartedly willing and ready from now on to live for him. Confident Christians are battleships surging through the waves. Timid Christians are little corks bobbing up and down and tossed around by every wind and tide. God wants our faith to be steeled with certainty. Romans 8 reasons with us with that aim in view, arguing that God loves us with an

1. Cf. Philip Schaff, editor, *The Creeds of Christendom* (Grand Rapids, 1990 reprint), I:534.
2. *Ecumenical Creeds and Reformed Confessions* (Grand Rapids, 1984), page 7.

invincible love. And when by faith we feel the certainty of his saving love, we are emboldened to live for him.

In verses 14-16 Paul identifies three ways we can know for sure that God loves us, three warrants for assurance of our salvation. And the interesting thing is not only what Paul does say, but also what he does not say. If we were to ask, 'How do I know for certain that I am a child of God?,' we might answer, 'I've put my faith in Christ.' At one level, that is valid. But we need more assurance than our own faith can give us. After all, how do we know that our faith is real enough and pure enough? We shouldn't put our faith in our faith.

Nor does Paul answer the question of assurance in terms of our doctrinal opinions. Having a theology more accurate than the next believer's theology is no warrant for assurance of salvation. My point is, if we look for assurance in terms of ourselves, we will never know with certainty. That is why Paul answers the question of assurance differently. He argues *God's* initiative toward us. He offers three grounds for confidence. Each is God-given, and each is experiential.

First, God's children are led by God's Spirit: 'For all who are led by the Spirit of God are sons of God' (verse 14). But what does it mean to be 'led by the Spirit'? The word 'For' at the beginning of our verse connects this 'being led' with 'putting to death the deeds of the body' back in verse 13. Being led by the Spirit and mortifying our sins by the Spirit are two complementary ways of describing the same thing. But Paul adds a new insight here in verse 14. Mortifying our sins by the Spirit generates Spirit-led forward movement in our Christian life. God leads us along step by step into ever richer and deeper life through mortification. The Christian experience is not a static state but an ongoing pilgrimage, as the Spirit leads us to put to death specific sins here and there in our personalities and finances and schedules and relationships and goals, and so forth. God knows better than we do where we need to move forward into deeper life by dying to ourselves. So he puts his finger on this and then on that, giving us the courage to keep moving forward, one step at a time. And Paul is saying that that progress in sanctification is how we prove that we really are 'sons of God'. God's true children are growing and changing and seeing things in a new way.

Have you gotten bogged down? If you have, some sin may be clogging up the work of God in your life. Ask God to show it to you. Go to God, hang on and do not let him go until he blesses you at your point of stagnancy. And when he does deal with you, trust him enough to accept his remedy. If some sin is holding you back, it is strong probably because for a long time you have felt a need for it. There is a reason why you have clung to it. But whatever that reason may be, your sin is a devil-shaped remedy that you are trying to force onto a God-shaped need. Only God can satisfy you. So trust him. Trust him so much that you get rid of your false remedy and open your heart to his leading and his answer. He wants to help you to mortify your (perhaps unintended) God-neglect by the power of his Spirit so that you can demonstrate that you are a true child of God.

Why is it that too many Christians live in a demoralizing mediocrity? Why is it that at our greatest points of need we may receive the least amount of divine power? The leading of the Holy Spirit into transformation is not some closely guarded secret. It is not meant only for a privileged élite. It is the inheritance of all of God's children. 1,600 years ago Augustine struggled with the question of human motivation. He wrote this:

> Give me a man in love. He knows what I mean. Give me one who yearns. Give me one who is hungry. Give me one, far away in this desert, who is thirsty and sighs for the spring of the Eternal country. Give me that sort of man. He knows what

I mean. But if I speak to a cold man, he just does not know what I am talking about.[3]

Augustine understood that the spring of authentic Christianity is not simply in the notions of our heads or in the choices of our wills. If we are applying the gospel only to those domains within, we should not be surprised if we are not getting the traction we need for forward movement. The spring of Christian power runs all the way down to what we *desire*. Most of what we do in life, we do out of the desires of our hearts. This is humbling, but true. So the more our hearts love the Lord, the more progress we will make.

But then we are confronted with a problem. How can we change our hearts? If we do desire to live fully for the Lord, then we are already on our way. But if we do not want to live fully for him, then we are stuck, aren't we? How can we desire what we do not even want to desire? How can we love what we do not even want to love? It is like trying to jump out of a hole that has no bottom. We are so enfeebled by sin that we cannot even determine for ourselves what our hearts will run after. And until we become 'men in love', as Augustine put it, how can we be led forward by the Spirit?

Consider the mercy of God! He meets us even at this level. Do you feel in your heart the slightest twinge of yearning to be God's man or God's woman from head to toe? 'A smoldering wick he will not snuff out' (Isaiah 42:3, NIV). God is able to fan into flame even our cold desires. He is able to win our unwilling hearts. When C. S. Lewis, as a new Christian, knelt in prayer for the first time, he was that night, according to his own report, 'the most dejected and reluctant convert in all England.'[4] What humility there is in God, that

---

3. Cf. Peter Brown, *Augustine of Hippo* (Berkeley, 1967), page 375.

4. C. S. Lewis, *Surprised by Joy: The Shape of My Early Life* (New York, 1955), pages 228-229.

he receives us on such terms and works with us even in that condition!

If your heart is cold toward God, he does not despise you. He knows your need before you ask. Hand yourself over to him just as you are and let him show you his reviving mercies. Augustus Toplady speaks for us all in his hymn:

Holy Ghost, dispel our sadness;
    pierce the clouds of sinful night;
come, thou source of sweetest gladness;
    breathe thy life and spread thy light.

Make that the prayer of your heart. God never lets faith go unmet. If you seek him according to his Word, you will find him. And you will discover warrant in your own experience for joyful assurance that he has made you his own dear child.

Our second warrant for assurance of salvation is that God's children have been psychologically liberated from dread and have begun to taste delight: 'For you did not receive the spirit of slavery to fall back into fear, but you have received the Spirit of adoption as sons, by whom we cry, 'Abba! Father!'' (verse 15). Through Christ, we enter into a new relationship with God – not only a new theology, but also a new relational nearness. We begin to live in the atmosphere of prayerful intimacy with God. No longer is God the dreaded slave-master we thought he was. That fear drove us from him. We hid from him, even as we may have dutifully attended church. And that sense of failure and rejection and distance hardens the heart. But the Holy Spirit of adoption, the Spirit of acceptance and overflowing love, enables us to perceive God as our dear heavenly Father. And Paul's point is that the Spirit gives us this new tenderness toward God to make us confident of our salvation.

When I was in sixth grade – just after the end of the last Ice Age! – Mr. Rhodes was my principal at Allandale

Elementary School in Pasadena, California. One day I was out in the hallways, doing something typically naughty, when I saw Mr. Rhodes come around the corner and head my way. I ducked into a hiding place while the danger passed by. But as I crouched there in fear, a solemn adult face suddenly loomed over me. It was Mr. Rhodes! I was caught. Now consider this. The very same man at the end of that day got into his car, drove home, walked into his house and said to his two daughters, 'Hi, kids.' They said, 'Hi, dad.' Doubtless, it was all very comfortable, familiar and sweet. Two very different perceptions of the same man! Servile fear and anxious dread *versus* childlike ease and strong loyalty. What made the difference? They were his children.

If you are in Christ, then you are God's dear child. And he has given you the Spirit of adoption, encouraging you to perceive God in a whole new way. God does not want you to be cringing in dread. He wants you to feel loved, because assurance is the relational atmosphere in which holiness can thrive.

In one sense, of course, God's children should always fear him. The fear of the Lord is the beginning of wisdom (Proverbs 9:10). But there is a *kind* of fear that God's children forever leave behind when he adopts them as his own. A cowering fear, a hesitancy, an insecurity – that is the mentality of a slave, not a son. But when God justifies us, he also adopts us as his children and sends his Spirit into our hearts, imparting a new confidence, a new sense of belonging. We finally see God as he is. Crying 'Abba! Father!' – that is what justification *feels* like. That is how justification connects with our actual experience. How beautiful this is. You do not need a Ph.D. in theology to cry 'Abba! Father!' You only need the Spirit of adoption.

The word 'Abba' was the Aramaic word that children in Paul's day used when addressing their fathers. Even Jesus prayed this way. In fact, Jesus is the one who taught us all to pray this way. He called God 'Abba, Father' even in the Garden of Gethsemane, at the worst moment of his life (Mark 14:36). It is the language of Jesus himself that Paul is repeating here. In the time of Jesus, Jewish religious culture did not encourage intimacy with God. It was customary among the Jews not to say God's name at all. When the Old Testament was read in the synagogue, and the passage included the divine name Yahweh (translated as 'the LORD' in our English Bibles), the reader did not come out and say 'Yahweh'. He did not want to risk taking God's name in vain. So the reader substituted the title 'Lord' for the name 'Yahweh' out of reverence for God. Jewish liturgy created a sense of distance from God. But Jesus changed all that. The Son of God invites us into intimacy with God as sons. This is why Paul writes elsewhere, 'Because you are sons, God sent the Spirit *of his Son* into our hearts, the Spirit who calls out, 'Abba, Father" (Galatians 4:6, NIV). And Jesus invites us to draw near to God the way he himself did: 'This is how you should pray: 'Our Father . . ." (Matthew 6:9)

There is a kind of reverence which is, in fact, irreverence. There is a way of putting God off at a distance which may look pious, but it is contrary to the will of God himself. There is a way of praying that is too formal and just pompous. What if my son Gavin called me 'Pastor Ortlund'? I would be offended. I would say, 'Son, I'm your dad. Yes, I'm also your pastor. But just call me dad.' And if he said to me, 'But Pastor, I want to be respectful of you,' I'd say, 'But I don't want that *kind* of respect. More than anything else, I'm your dad. And I want no barriers between us.' And so it is with God. It is not reverent to erect barriers of icy formality which Jesus died to tear down. Doing so is pious rebellion. There is no more beautiful reverence in the sight of God than the simple heartcry, 'Abba! Father!'

Our third ground for confidence is that God's children receive the witness of the Holy Spirit to their own spirits that they belong to God: 'The Spirit himself bears witness with our spirit that we are children of God' (verse 16). According to verse 15, our hearts cry out to God. But verse 16 is even more profound. The Spirit himself bears witness to our spirits. This is a mystery, but very real and wonderful. The third warrant for assurance of salvation is the personal touch of God in the depths of your being.

The witness of the Spirit to your spirit is not an inference you draw from an argument. It is a clear and distinct experience of God. When I walk under the warmth of the Georgia sun, I do not ask, 'By what line of reasoning may I conclude that this sunlight is falling on me?' I just know it is. It is too obvious to doubt. Indeed, it is that sunlight that enables me to see everything else. And when the Holy Spirit breathes assurances to your spirit that you are God's child, his testimony carries a certainty that needs no validation. That witness itself becomes the support and encouragement by which everything hopeful in your life can then spring forth.

The witness of the Spirit is not a message from God that no one but you will ever know. It is not special revelation. But God is able to pour his felt love into our hearts through the Holy Spirit (Romans 5:5). And this is normative Christian experience, not the private reserve of a privileged élite.

God's people through the ages have known such assurance. We cannot stereotype the ways of God with the soul. The Spirit's testimony varies from person to person. But God does give something of this privilege to all his children. Sarah Edwards, the wife of Jonathan Edwards, left a record of this work of God in her own heart. She had struggled with a sense of God's wrath upon her. But he took it away:

I felt a strong desire to be alone with God, to go to him, without having anyone to interrupt the silent and soft communion which I earnestly desired between God and my own soul, and accordingly withdrew to my chamber. . . . [She read Romans 8 in her Bible at this point.] The words . . . appeared to me with undoubted certainty as the words of God, and as words which God did pronounce concerning me. I had no more doubt of it than I had of my being. I seemed, as it were, to hear the great God proclaiming thus to the world concerning me, 'Who shall lay anything to thy charge?' It was strongly impressed upon me how impossible it was for anything in heaven or earth, in this world or the future, ever to separate me from the love of God which is in Christ Jesus. I cannot find language to express how certain this appeared – the everlasting mountains and hills were but shadows to it. My safety and happiness and eternal enjoyment of God's unchanging love seemed as durable and unchangeable as God himself. Melted and overcome by the sweetness of this assurance, I fell into a great flow of tears and could not help weeping aloud.[5]

The intensity of the Spirit's witness varies from occasion to occasion and from person to person. The Holy Spirit of God cannot be standardized. But what difference would it make, as we struggle and suffer and serve and die, to live often in the felt love of God? What would that be worth? Would that be helpful, as we go through life's troubles? For example, are you widowed or divorced? You always have One nearer to you than even when you had your own spouse. And when you lie awake at night alone in your bed, your eternal Companion knows how to testify to your spirit that you are God's dear child. Are you married – and discouraged? This is where the renewal of your marriage begins – not in communication skills and negotiations with your spouse, valid

5. *The Works of Jonathan Edwards* (Edinburgh, 1979 reprint), I:lxii-lxiii. Edited slightly for style.

as that is, but with your own heart bathed and healed in the
love of God. Wouldn't that make a difference? Wouldn't it
help if the mountains of frost and ice within you began to
melt in the warmth of the overflowing love of God? Or are
you a young person? God did not create you to be weary
with life when you're only nineteen. But if you've watched
so many trashy videos and exposed yourself to so much
garbage that you're already desensitized and bored, you can
be made young again and you can stay young – in the nearness
of God, where he will show you depths of his love you've
never dreamed existed.

Charles Haddon Spurgeon, the nineteenth-century British
preacher, counseled his people this way:

> If you have a desire, God has given it to you. If you pant and
> cry and groan for Christ, even this is his gift. Bless him for it.
> Thank him for little grace, and ask him for great grace. He has
> given you hope, ask for faith. And when he gives you faith,
> ask for assurance. And when you get assurance, ask for full
> assurance. And when you have obtained full assurance, ask for
> enjoyment. And when you have enjoyment, ask for glory itself.
> And he will surely give it to you in his own appointed season.[6]

As the Holy Spirit leads you along, as he helps you by
faith to cry 'Abba! Father!' and himself whispers to your
spirit, 'I am your salvation' (Psalm 35:3) – when God wants
to give you assurance in his simple and humble way, do not
harden your heart. The felt love of God energizes bold
Christian living. Whether in joy or in sorrow, strong personal
assurance of salvation is what causes your inner nuclear
reactor to reach critical mass, so that all sorts of wonderful,
sin-expelling, God-honoring effects are generated.

---

6. C. H. Spurgeon, *Revival Year Sermons: 1859* (Edinburgh, 1959),
page 77. Edited slightly for clarity.

Will you open your heart to receive these gifts of God? Prepare yourself in three ways. One, humble yourself. Jesus said, 'Blessed are the poor in spirit' (Matthew 5:3). Stoop low enough to drink from the river of the water of life that flows from the throne of God (Revelation 22:1). No sin is so Spirit-quenching as pride.

Two, clear away clutter from your soul. Paul said, 'I consider everything rubbish, that I may gain Christ and be found in him' (Philippians 3:7-9, NIV). What is competing with Jesus for the place of supremacy in your heart? Get rid of it. Do you love money more than him? Some of us would be greatly liberated by giving away a huge amount of our money. Do you love your children more than the Lord? That is unfair to them and soul-damaging to you. Do you draw your significance and identity from your work? Smash that idol. Prepare the way of the Lord into your soul.

Three, seek him. There is, as it were, a light switch deep inside you, the switch of certainty. It is so deep inside you that you cannot even reach down inside yourself to turn that light on. Only God can. And he really can. So go out of your usual way to tell God that you mean business with him, that you will not let him go until he blesses you. He says, 'You will seek me and you will find me, when you seek me with all your heart' (Jeremiah 29:13). He is not an unanswering God. He is there. He is there for you.

Chapter Seven

Suffering and Glory

[17] . . . and if children, then heirs – heirs of God and fellow heirs with Christ, provided we suffer with him in order that we may also be glorified with him. [18] For I consider that the sufferings of this present time are not worth comparing with the glory that is to be revealed to us.

In my boyhood years, our family took summer vacations on the beach at Cape Cod, Massachusetts. Dad and Mom enjoyed the rest, my sisters enjoyed the sun, but that wasn't the favorite part of it for me. My favorite part was watching World War III every day. You see, the military had grounded an old battleship some distance offshore. And every day warplanes flew low overhead, right over our beach, to strafe that ship. They released their rockets just overhead and I could follow the shot all the way to that ship and – kaboom! – assess their accuracy. Every day they put on a war just for me. What more could an eight-year-old boy ask for?

But I wonder if some Christians are like that grounded ship. They can't seem to get going. They are stuck where they are. And they become target practice for the enemy of their souls. What do those Christians need? Do they need to be told that they should be better Christians? They already know that. What do they need? They need the tide to rise. They need the currents of faith and hope and love to rise and swell in their hearts. They need to float again. Then they can move – without having to be dragged along.

In Romans chapter 8 Paul is declaring what God has done to get us floating in the tides of faith, hope and love in the Holy Spirit. These godly affections lifting our hearts accomplish what the law by itself could never do. In verses 17-18, we see the heart-lifting power of hope.

Despair is the atmosphere in which most people live today. Their despair does not take the form of weeping and wailing. But they possess nothing that this life will not eventually crush, and they know it. A dull ache rather than acute pain is the symptom of today's despair. Years ago Peggy Lee came out with a song entitled, 'Is that all there is?' It was a bouncy tune, but Despair wrote the words:

Is that all there is? Is that all there is?
Then let's keep dancing, let's break out the booze and have a ball,
if that's all there is.

Between that refrain she narrated the landmark experiences
in her life – falling in love, her house burning down, and so
forth. She expected these experiences somehow to take her
to finality. But she kept asking, 'Is that all there is? Is that all
there is to love, to a fire? *That's* all there is to these intense
moments in life?' Clearly, she would never find an experience
that would not cause her to ask, 'Is that all there is?' The
malaise of despair is rarely defined so clearly.

One can sympathize. This mortal life *is* pervasively
disappointing. 'From the best bliss that earth imparts, we turn
unfilled to thee again,' wrote Bernard of Clairvaux many
centuries ago. But then *why* do we feel disappointed? *Why*
do we feel unfilled? Because we were made for something
better than this life, and we all know it deep inside. If we feel
a desire that nothing in this world can satisfy, doesn't that
imply that we weren't made for this world?[1] This life is not
meant to satisfy us but to arouse us, to kindle in us a passion
for the solid joys and lasting treasures in God's presence.
And when that hope begins to resonate in our hearts, when
our hearts are lifted up beyond this present evil age, our
transformation begins.

We can be glad that this is the apostle Paul speaking to us
about suffering and hope. The man is qualified. He suffered.
Yet he also said with convincing authenticity, 'I *rejoice* in
my sufferings for you' (Colossians 1:24, NIV). No self-pity.
No mock heroics. His whole persona bears witness to the
transforming power of hope. He discovered in his afflictions,
and he teaches us to find in ours, warrant for assurance of

----

1. Cf. C. S. Lewis, *Mere Christianity* (New York, 1958), page 106.

salvation (verse 17) and a staggering insight into the value of our future glory (verse 18).

'. . . and if children, then heirs – heirs of God and fellow heirs with Christ' (verse 17a). According to verse 16, the Spirit assures us that we are God's children. But what is that worth to us? Being his children – just being his children, not even being his 'good' children – that is what opens eternity up! Your eternal happiness hinges on this one thing: Are you a child of God? The question is worth asking, because 'if children, then heirs.' It is as if God has made up a will – not that he's going to die, but he *has* provided for the future of his children. 'If children, then heirs.'

Heirs of what? 'Heirs of God.' That means two things. First, we stand to inherit eternal joys. Ultimately, in heaven, God will wipe all tears from our eyes, and the old order of things will forever pass away (Revelation 21:4). We ourselves will be like Jesus, each of us in his own way, at the most authentic and spontaneous depth of our natural personalities (1 John 3:1-2). We have 'an eternal house' in heaven (2 Corinthians 5:1). We have an inheritance 'incorruptible, undefiled, unfading' (1 Peter 1:4). So heaven will not disappoint us as this life does. All of God's promises will pour into our laps with a potency of joy we were created for but have never yet tasted.

Secondly, 'heirs of God' means that we stand to inherit God himself. This is where the hope of the gospel really transforms. If we are devastated by earthly loss, it reveals that we have been living for earthly gain. But, though we feel the buffetings of life as keenly as anyone, being an heir of God means we no longer sulk over earthly loss. We treasure God as our eternal inheritance. We not only *trust* God, we also *value* God as our dearest desire:

Whom have I in heaven but you?
And earth has nothing I desire besides you.
My flesh and my heart may fail,
but God is the strength of my heart
and my portion for ever. Psalm 73:25-26, NIV

'The LORD is my portion,' says my soul; therefore I will hope in him' (Lamentations 3:24, RSV). 'I desire to depart and be with Christ, which is better by far' (Philippians 1:23, NIV).

Here is the question every one of us asks: What is *my* chance for happiness? What is *my* slice of the pie? And here is the Christian's answer: *The Lord is my portion*. If you are an heir of God, if you are his and he is yours, if you will spend eternity exploring the infinite vastness of the wisdom and goodness and joy and power and love of your holy God, then you have indestructible, indescribable happiness. And right now the gospel renews you as you savor the value of your inheritance.

Recently a suffering friend said to me, 'What else is God going to take away from me? He's taken so much. What's next?' God may take it all away. In fact, he surely will. 'Naked I came from my mother's womb, and naked I will depart,' Job said (Job 1:21, NIV). Someday every one of us will be completely stripped of our little earthly all. In the last several years members of our church have died of cancer, stroke, an airplane wreck, complications from diabetes, choking, a motorcycle accident and, of course, old age. As George Bernard Shaw said, 'One out of one dies.' Somehow or other, every one of us will die. And the earthly life we have labored to build will turn to dust. So what does that leave us with? If on our final day we possess this one thing only – God himself – if we have his promises and his approval, will we be rich, or will we be poor? If God possesses all things, and if we inherit God, then we will inherit all things. Isn't that worth suffering for now? Isn't that worth *anything* now? Are we forsaken, if we suffer loss to gain Christ? If, when everything temporal is forever taken away from us and everything eternal is finally given to us, so that all we end up with is an 'eternal weight of glory' (2 Corinthians 4:17), will God have treated us poorly? Lift up your heart! Your life is not shutting down. It has barely begun.

And not only are we heirs of God, we are also 'fellow heirs with Christ.' If God is our Father, then Christ is our brother and we are his fellow heirs. Let this sink in. Hebrews 1:2 says that Jesus is the 'heir of all things.' He owns everything. He has the rights to everything, simply everything. God has given him all authority in heaven and on earth. And he has made us his partners in his final triumph. All that is his by right he will share with us by grace. Someday, perhaps very soon, he will open the door and say to us, 'Enter into the joy of your master' (Matthew 25:21). So if we are fellow heirs with Christ, then our inheritance is as secure and as glorious and as joyful as his inheritance. Isn't this what Jesus prayed for, when he asked the Father that we would be with him and see his glory (John 17:24)? You and I are going to be there.

But then Paul adds a searching qualification: 'provided we suffer with him in order that we may also be glorified with him' (verse 17b). Why does Paul say that? Because we might shrink from sharing in Christ's sufferings. But what a miscalculation that would be! Paul is still talking about assurance of salvation. And a true Christian shares in the sufferings of Christ. A true Christian drinks from the cup he drank from. A true Christian humbles himself and obeys the Father, the way Jesus did. Our Lord said, 'Take up your cross every day and follow me' (Luke 9:23). Paul set an example of sharing in Christ's sufferings and becoming like him in his death (Philippians 3:10). The author of Hebrews calls us to 'go to [Jesus] outside the camp, bearing the disgrace he bore' (Hebrews 13:13). Peter said, 'Rejoice that you participate in the sufferings of Christ, so that you may be overjoyed when his glory is revealed' (1 Peter 4:13).

God's children have always suffered with Christ. They have embraced his cross. They have obeyed him in hard ways. Not all have been martyrs. But for all of us there will be suffering in this present evil age, because the world loves God no more now than when they crucified Jesus. And if we are living each day in simple obedience, we will feel deep but holy sufferings. But we are glad to. After all, we are going to give ourselves to something. Why not something beautiful, that lasts forever? In fact, Christians *choose* to suffer. We walk right into it with eyes wide open to the price we will pay. Why? Because we are not *just* suffering. We are sharing in *his* sufferings. We are bringing the love of Christ into hostile territory where it needs to be seen and felt. That is what Jesus did, and following him is a privilege. So we do not feel sorry for ourselves. The Bible says, 'If we died with him, we will also live with him; if we endure, we will also reign with him' (2 Timothy 2:11-12).

Suffering does not earn us any glory. Jesus earned glory for us through his own meritorious sufferings. But our sufferings are meaningful preparation for glory. Pain burns the superficiality out of us. We stop caring about all the wrong things. We are released from bondage to earthly imperatives and intensified in our yearnings for eternal things. In suffering, we can discover how sweet God really is.

Now do you see, in verse 17, how deftly Paul transitions from our inheritance to our glory? He does not say what we expect him to say. We expect him to say, 'provided we suffer with him in order that we may also *inherit* with him.' But instead, Paul says, 'in order that we may also *be glorified* with him.' Why? Because the metaphor of inheritance is inadequate. It only goes so far. And step by step in Romans 8

Paul is lifting our vision to ultimacy. Yes, we have an inheritance in God. But it is not like any earthly 'inheritance'. No earthly metaphor can do justice to what our Father and our Brother plan to share with us. So Paul takes us to the next level with the word *glory*.

We do wonder, 'I'm paying a price to obey God. *Is it worth it?*' We reason. We measure. We calculate – more than we may admit. But Paul is not embarrassed to admit his own calculating. He comes right out and says in verse 18, 'I consider, I figure, I reckon, I calculate, I've done the math – and I know that the sufferings of this present time are not worth comparing with the glory that is to be revealed to us.' If we think of our future reward only in terms of an 'inheritance', our earthliness might drag our prophetic vision down so low that hope loses its transforming power. We have to get all financial equations out of our heads so that we never think, 'Well, frankly, for a million dollars I *would* commit sin X,' or, 'For an earthly reward, I *will* keep quiet about Jesus.' But if our inheritance is not of an earthly nature, if our inheritance is of the nature of *glory*, then all worldly evaluations become irrelevant. And *that* hope has the power to transform us.

In 2 Corinthians 4:17 Paul says that our present sufferings are achieving for us 'an eternal weight of glory'. That is what glory is. It is weightiness, density, solidity. This life is thin and pale and shadowy. From the beginning, the devil has been telling us that sin is life's high octane added ingredient, to turbo-charge our experience. But show me one human life where that has actually worked out. Show me one human life devoted to sin that has turned out to be the life *you* long for. Sin does not add substance. It dilutes life. It waters down our experience. It leaves a bitter after-taste. It hollows us out so that we start wondering, 'Is that all there is?' Look around at our society. As people become more empty and bored and restless, is it because everyone is becoming more Christian? We were not made for sin. We were made to become solid, natural human beings sharing in the awesome, supernatural glory of Christ – men and women to be reckoned with.

God takes us more seriously than we take ourselves. We trivialize our existence, but God plans to *glorify* us. We have more significance than we realize, more than we sometimes want. In any case, God's promise of glory here in Romans 8:18 shows how pathetic 'fire-insurance Christianity' really is – accepting Jesus just to stay out of hell. God's plan is not just to keep us out of hell. God's plan is to make us glorious like Christ.

And what Paul wants us to see, so that hope will exert its transforming power, is how *light* our present afflictions are compared with that eternal weight of glory. Isn't that beautiful? Paul does not say, 'Being God's child entails suffering. Accept it.' He says, 'Being God's child entails suffering. Now let me explain why it's *worth* accepting.' And the reason is this. God will not compensate you for the price you pay to follow Jesus. God will not do that – one-for-one reimbursement for what we have to endure in this life. God, who will be no man's debtor, plans to open up the floodgates and pour out upon you blessing and favor and privilege and pleasure and delight and endless discovery out of all proportion to the price you have paid. Paul is not slighting our sufferings. But he is saying that, *compared with our glorious inheritance*, they really are endurable.

And our glory is not far away, off in the remote future.[2]

---

2. Paul's unusual wording may suggest, beyond the obvious futurity, certainty and/or imminence as well. William Arndt and F. Wilbur Gingrich, *A Greek-English Lexicon of the New Testament* (Chicago, 1969 reprint), s.v. μέλλω, interpret our text as connoting imminence: 'be on the point of, be about to.'

You are only a heartbeat away from it. If 'the worst' should happen, you graduate to glory sooner rather than later. The nations of the world will fade into nothing, but you will live on. When the sun finally burns out, you will be just beginning. Right now you receive your life from God indirectly through food. Prior to that, life came to you filtered through the past thousand-plus generations of your ancestors. But then, in glory, you will receive your life directly from the face of God in wave after unending wave of the life that is truly life. Right now we relish the small pleasures that God has placed down here inside nature. But what will it be like to be there with him, drinking forever from the Fountainhead, swimming in the ocean of God's love and never touching bottom?

So what is God's promise of glory worth? Let your life declare it. If you do not declare the supreme value of your glorious inheritance, you will surely declare the supreme value of your earthly comfort and popularity and self-preservation and all the other degrading values that make people light and insubstantial. Peter Kreeft helps us to savor the power of this when he writes:

Spiritual death means hell. Now suppose both death and hell were utterly defeated. Suppose the fight was fixed. Suppose God took you on a crystal ball trip into your future and you saw with indubitable certainty that despite everything – your sin, your smallness, your stupidity – you could have free for the asking your whole crazy heart's deepest desire: heaven, eternal joy. Would you not return fearless and singing? What can earth do to you if you are guaranteed heaven? To fear the worst earthly loss would be like a millionaire fearing the loss of a penny – less, a scratch on a penny.[3]

---

3. Peter Kreeft, *Heaven: The Heart's Deepest Longing* (San Francisco, 1980), page 183.

Until we are glorified with the Lord, the cross will come before the crown. And tomorrow morning you and I will go back to work. But if the hope of glory throbs in our hearts, we will go to work transformed. We will be available to our Lord to demonstrate his supreme value among people who are in bondage to this earth. And we will prove his worth by paying a price to live for him, with no sense of melodrama but with a quiet sense of privilege, because sharing in his glory is worth *everything*.

Chapter Eight

The Creation Set Free

[19]For the creation waits with eager longing for the revealing of the sons of God. [20]For the creation was subjected to futility, not willingly, but because of him who subjected it, in hope [21] that the creation itself will be set free from its bondage to decay and obtain the freedom of the glory of the children of God.

The devil wants to destroy our faith. He wants to grind us down until we give up on God. He tried with Job (Job 1:1-2:10) and Jesus (Matthew 4:1-11) and Peter (Luke 22:31-32), and he tries with us too. But God aims to deepen and expand our faith with a growing expectancy and resilient joy. He does that by equipping our faith with great promises.

How big are the promises of God? What do God's children stand to inherit? Is our inheritance grand enough to thrill our hearts and deserve our all? Or is Christian faith just a religious garnish on the side of a life of demoralized mediocrity? In verses 19-21, Paul shows us the *grandeur* of God's redemptive purpose. He aims to kindle in our hearts a new sense of destiny, of greatness, of expectancy, so that we bank all our happiness forever on God – with all the radical entailments of such confidence now.

In Romans 8:18 Paul dares to tell us, 'Our present cancer and persecution and financial losses and loneliness and death – our present sufferings are *not worth comparing* with the glory that is to be revealed to us.' And deep down inside we say, 'Okay, I know I'm supposed to agree with that, because it's in the Bible. But do I *really* believe it? There is a limit to how far I'll go with Jesus. It doesn't take much adversity for my faith to start wavering. Are God's promises really worth *this* life I'm stuck with?' If our present sufferings are not worth comparing with the glory to be revealed to us, *by what standard of measurement* is that so? Our sufferings seem so overwhelming, maybe the most faithful response our hearts can manage is, 'Tell me more about this glory. How big is it, Paul? Tell me more.' So he does, in verses 19-21. With prophetic vision, the apostle explains that God's promises include the whole creation in their redemptive scope. That is how big the promised glory really is. The whole creation is our standard for measuring our coming glory.

Paul helps us to perceive creation in its present condition

with new eyes. This whole context in which we presently live is not normal. It is not the measure of what God can do. It has been 'subjected to futility' – and that, 'not willingly' (verse 20). The created order right now is like a coil spring tightly compressed, straining to be released. J. B. Phillips uses another metaphor: 'The whole creation is on tiptoe to see the wonderful sight of the sons of God coming into their own' (verse 19). The Greek scholar, James Hope Moulton, proposed that the unusual word, translated 'eager longing' in the ESV, may suggest the idea of someone craning his neck, stretching his head, in eager anticipation to see what is coming.[1] And if the creation can hardly wait for what is coming next, how can we sit back in complacency? The future God has promised us is cosmic in scope and royal in elevation.

Astonishingly, the creation yearns for us rulers of creation to be restored to our original greatness. Genesis 1:26-28 teaches that God made us the crown of creation – and a glorious creation, too, not the broken down old creation we live in now. But Romans 8 envisions the world renovated with perfection and released into our possession. And the creation itself yearns for the day.

But in what sense does the creation 'wait with eager longing' for our debut as the glorified children of God? Is Paul saying that the robins and oak trees and largemouth bass and the Matterhorn are actually feeling and thinking this way? I doubt it. Paul is speaking figuratively. He is personifying the creation.[2] So what does he mean?

---

1. James Hope Moulton and Wilbert Francis Howard, *A Grammar of New Testament Greek, Volume II: Accidence and Word Formation* (Edinburgh, 1968 reprint), page 274. Cf. Douglas J. Moo, *The Epistle to the Romans* (Grand Rapids, 1996), page 513.

2. Marcus L. Loane, *The Hope of Glory* (Waco, 1968), page 81: 'Thus he ascribed to it the force of a hidden language and he discerned in it the voice of a buried anguish.'

Remember that, in the beginning, God pronounced the newly created cosmos 'very good' (Genesis 1:31). And for *God* to call something very good means a lot! The creation must have been spectacular. But then we sinned. And God judged. His curse upon the ground subjected the creation to futility (Genesis 3:17-19). Do you remember that line in the hymn 'Abide with me'? 'Change and decay in all around I see.' *Change and decay*. That's the way life is, isn't it? We just cannot hang onto it. The creation is not working – not the way it was meant to, anyway.

We have difficulty imagining how the creation was designed to perform. We have never seen what it can do. Steve Green sings a song entitled 'Symphony of Praise' with these words:

The Composer and Conductor of the universe
steps before the orchestra of God
creation lifts their finely crafted instruments
as all in heaven wildly applaud

The seasons well rehearsed begin with his downbeat
and on his cue the sun trumpets the dawn
the whirling winds swell in a mighty crescendo
with each commanding sweep of his baton
the oceans pound the shore in march to his cadence
the galaxies all revolve in cosmic rhyme
the fall of raindrops all in wild syncopation
as lightning strikes and thunder claps in time

The symphony of praise
conducted by the Ancient of Days
may each creation great or small
lift their voices one and all
in the symphony of praise

This cosmic orchestra can perform beyond our capacity to imagine. God never creates mediocrity. He made the creation capable of broadcasting *huge volumes* of praise back to himself. But we have never heard the creation pull out all the stops. We have never heard it echo praises back to God as it was designed to do and even now is capable of doing. Why? Because when man sinned in the Garden of Eden and we fell from our place of glorious dominion, God said to his whole creation, 'Shhh. Not yet.'

And that is why it has long appeared to perceptive people that this world is all for nothing. Think of the books, the movies, the poetry, agonizing over life's futility. That anguish is not unbelief. It is true. The symphony of praise *has* been muted. God's handiwork *is* allowed to crumble into dust. The creation is pervaded with corruption and death – but not because of any flaw in its design or its own intrinsic nature ('not willingly'). God himself has imposed upon his awesome creation a temporary restraining order ('him who subjected it'). The trouble in the world is not due merely to human pollution and destruction. More profoundly, God himself, with all his judicial power, has decreed the temporary reign of futility ('bondage to decay').

But futility is not God's final word: 'For the creation was subjected to futility . . . *in hope* that the creation itself will be set free' (verses 20-21a). Hope and release have been God's aim all along. And when God's purpose for this fractured world has been accomplished, then we, his children, will enter into our glorious freedom. God will take the lid off and the whole universe will burst forth with joy and freshness. We will go out in joy and be led forth in peace. The mountains and hills before us shall break forth into singing, and all the trees of the field shall clap their hands, as Isaiah 55 prophesies. 'The creation itself will be set free from its bondage to decay and obtain the freedom of the glory of the children of God,'

Paul writes. And you and I, whom God has adopted to inherit his loving intentions, will be there to experience it.

How grand is the scope of the gospel! How sweeping its relevance! God is so imaginative, so bold, so full of wonderful ideas. His gospel is so magnificent. By contrast, as I write, the 2000 presidential election in the United States is heating up. But I notice that the mountains and hills are *not* breaking forth into singing. How pathetic are all human gospels. They have no ultimate answers, no final hope beyond tinkering with the problems of this life. Woody Allen does not have any answers, either, but he can ask some good questions:

I always see the death's head lurking. I could be sitting at Madison Square Garden at the most exciting basketball game, and they're cheering and everything is thrilling, and one of the players is doing something very beautiful – and my thought will be, 'He's only twenty-eight years old and I only wish he could savor this moment in some way, because, you know, this is as good as it's going to get for him.' . . . The fundamental thing behind all motivation and all activity is the constant struggle against annihilation and against death. It's absolutely stupefying in its terror, and it renders anyone's accomplishments meaningless. As Camus wrote, it's not only that *he* dies or that *man* does, but that you struggle to do a work of art that will last and then realize that *the universe itself* is not going to exist after a time. Until those issues are resolved within each person – religiously or psychologically or existentially – the social and political issues will never be resolved, except in a slapdash way.[3]

Woody Allen is right, which is why it is such a privilege for a believer to embrace the hope of the gospel. The gospel is more than we might have thought. It is not a private religious

---

3. F. Rich, 'Woody Allen Wipes the Smile off his Face,' *Esquire*, May 1977, pages 75f. Emphases his.

preference. It is nothing less than God's prophetic declaration of a new universe ruled by a new human race. So the question is not, Does the gospel promise enough to thrill our hearts? The question is, Does our faith have the elasticity to stretch out far enough to match the grandeur of the promises of God?

The gospel transforms us because the promises of God match the yearnings of our hearts perfectly. This is how God turns ordinary people into heroes. He has the nerve – if I may put it that way – to look us right in the eye and say, 'Your present sufferings are not worth comparing with what I'm planning for you in a renewed creation.' Who else can say that to us? Nobody else even thinks in those terms. Everybody else is offering us escape from our sufferings, but no one else is offering us an eternal hope infinitely greater than our sufferings. All human gospels are trivial and trivializing. But the bold magnitude of the promises of God makes following Jesus worth it all.

And God's promises also make our own small thinking inexcusable. In view of the massive goodness of God, the small-minded Christian is a living contradiction. Narrow-mindedness is a non-Christian mentality. Largeness of mind and spirit, largeness of scope and vision, largeness of expectations and faith – that is the Christian outlook. As Augustine said, 'It is yearning that makes the heart deep.'[4] The promises of God are calculated to deepen our hearts by quickening great yearnings within us. So when the grandeur of the Christian hope comes home to our hearts, all nit-picky legalism and foot-dragging complacency are seen to be absurd. The gospel spreads *magnificence* out before us. So away with our gloomy unbelief! Yes, we should weep with those who weep (Romans 12:15). We should be especially tender with those who struggle against chronic depression.

---

4. Cf. Peter Brown, *Augustine of Hippo* (Berkeley, 1967), page 156.

But our problems cannot be allowed to eclipse our hope. The gospel unveils a reality out beyond our sins and limitations, its glory undimmed by the weariness of this life and chemical disorder in our brains. The sheer objectivity of Joy leaves us with no choice but to put away our smallness and moroseness and by faith join the creation in its eager longing.

Romans 8 turns our eyes toward a world far better than this one, promised by God, soon to be revealed. But it is not streets of gold that we look forward to. God himself is the reward of our hearts. Verses 19-21 simply show that, if we will set our hearts on him, God will throw in a renewed creation as well. But if you look for your happiness to the world as it is now, you will end up with nothing.[5] And your life will be worth nothing. You will live out your days with one slapdash attempt at satisfaction after another, until Death lays down his trump card. So think. Respect your own happiness. Stake your all on the promises of God. Do not see your life now as the final measure of your happiness, your worth, your significance. This present life of sighs and groans will yield to shouts and dances. Let that certainty define you.

And when God does set the creation free, that delightful world will provide the venue in which we will experience the all-surpassing worth of being heirs of God. That vision is the standard by which we should measure whether the sufferings of this present time should be compared with the glory to be revealed to us. Jonathan Edwards saw it this way:

> To go to heaven, fully to enjoy God, is *infinitely* better than the most pleasant accommodations here. Fathers and mothers, husbands, wives or children or the company of earthly friends are but shadows; but the enjoyment of God is the substance. These are but the scattered beams; but God is the sun. These

5. Cf. C. S. Lewis, *Mere Christianity* (New York, 1958), page 104.

are but streams; but God is the fountain. These are but drops; but God is the ocean.[6]

So does the gospel promise you enough to live fully for Christ now? If your heart doesn't already know the answer, then you are still living in the outer darkness. But if your heart does relish the answer, then, for you, that eternal happiness has already begun.

6. *The Works of Jonathan Edwards* (Edinburgh, 1979), II:244. Emphasis his.

Chapter Nine

Groaning

[22] For we know that the whole creation has been groaning together in the pains of childbirth until now. [23] And not only the creation, but we ourselves, who have the first fruits of the Spirit, groan inwardly as we wait eagerly for adoption as sons, the redemption of our bodies. [24] For in this hope we were saved. Now hope that is seen is not hope. For who hopes for what he sees? [25] But if we hope for what we do not see, we wait for it with patience.

This life is not really life. Our present existence is a living death, and we are on our way to real life. Christians are people who find in their hearts such yearnings for true life, such confidence in God's promises of that life, that they face into their sufferings with a rugged determination to live well and die well now. Non-Christians are people, including church-going people, whose hearts are captivated by the rewards of this life. They do not suffer loss to gain Christ, because they do not value Christ. They may say that they have a 'relationship' with Jesus in some vague sense. But authentic Christianity is more than a relationship with Jesus in some vague sense. The Christianity that compels the attention of the world is prizing Jesus so much that one's way of calculating happiness is transformed. Gaining present rewards and escaping present miseries are no longer one's driving concerns. Escaping hell is not even one's primary concern. Christians are people for whom Jesus is so real and the prospect of inheriting true life from him is so awesome that they are transformed into future-oriented people. Pseudo-Christianity turns its face down into this world, like an animal at the trough. Real Christianity is drawn onward to a better world.[1] And if some people say, 'Your faith is just pie-in-the-sky by and by,' we say, 'Yes, you finally understand. Pie-in-the-sky by and by – that is precisely the transforming power of the gospel.'

Therefore, the most urgent question in our lives is not, 'What do we have? What do we have of this world's goods and honors and benefits?' Pseudo-Christianity never stops asking that question, hoping for God's help to get even more. But the question with which the Holy Spirit searches our hearts is, 'What would you *rather* have?' You and I need to

---

1. Cf. D. Martyn Lloyd-Jones, *Romans 8:17-39: The Final Perseverance of the Saints* (Edinburgh, 1975), page 104.

make up our minds. Will we nose into this world with the occasional glance upward, especially when we bite into something that tastes bad? Or will we bend our souls upward and onward to a better life promised by God? Which would we *rather* have? If we would rather have this present life, then we will be willing to lose Christ to gain the world. If we would rather have Christ, then we will be willing to lose all things to gain him. And we do not answer that question in our heads. We all know the 'right' answer in our heads. That question is inevitably answered deep in our hearts, where how we really feel cannot be denied.

God aims so to charm us and delight us and thrill us with his promises that our hearts say more meaningfully than ever before, 'I'd rather have Jesus than silver or gold, I'd rather be his than have riches untold, I'd rather have Jesus than anything this world affords today.' He wants so to coax us and win us and persuade us that our hearts say, 'Give me Jesus. You can have all this world, but give me Jesus.' When these powerful desires start to percolate in our hearts, we are transformed.

In this section of Romans 8, Paul is explaining how big God's promises really are.

In verse 17, 'provided we suffer with him' implies that suffering with Christ is an essential mark of the children of God. All people suffer. It is the universal consequence of sin, directly or indirectly. But God's children do not just suffer; they suffer *with Christ* by following him even when it is hard. The problem is, even God's children are weak and timid. How can we be fortified to follow Jesus wherever he leads? Starting at verse 18, Paul encourages us to follow Jesus at any cost. The glory to be revealed to us is so great that suffering now with him is a good deal, a privilege, the opportunity of a lifetime. The glory to be revealed to us is massive. The whole creation will be set free from its bondage to decay when you and I are promoted to our glory as children of God.

Would you like not only to be renewed yourself but also to live in a whole creation renewed with you, rejoicing with you in a freshness and youth and exuberance that will never become wearisome but only more delightful forever? Would you like to experience that? Would you like to retire there – forever, and forever young? Naturally! So, okay. Let's suffer with Christ now.

But let me point out something I have not yet made clear. Romans 8:18-25 is not about heaven, at least the way people often think of heaven – a place far away from here and totally different from this world. Paul is envisioning *the renewal of creation*, with our very bodies redeemed out of weary decrepitude into resurrection immortality. If you die in Christ, your personality, your spirit, your consciousness, goes immediately to be with the Lord (2 Corinthians 5:6, 8; Philippians 1:23). That confidence makes us strong. But God promises us even more than that. As Paul explains here, God promises us a renewed creation (Isaiah 65:17-25; Revelation 21:1-5) as the theater in which we will experience the eternal drama.

Do you notice that the word *heaven* nowhere appears in this passage, but the word *creation* appears four times (verses 19, 20, 21, 22)? In verse 23 Paul mentions our bodies as the final triumph of our redemption. So here is my point. The glory God promises us, the glory by which we should measure our present sufferings, is not an ethereal, unreal dream but a very recognizable reality. It is this creation right here right now, only renewed in perfection. Paul envisions the redemption of our bodies, these bodies right here right now. Look at your fingers. Look at your fingerprints. The FBI tells us that those swirls of lines on your fingers are unique to you. Do you realize that, changed into a glorious body (1

Corinthians 15:35-58), it is *these* God-created fingers that will leave your personal fingerprints all over the new heavens and the new earth? Everything suffering and death take away from us God will give back to us, and in better condition. So what do we have to lose, suffering with Christ?

In verse 23 Paul implies that the redemption of our bodies is something for which we may properly yearn. He is not thinking of our future glory in a cartoonish way, with you and me sitting on fluffy clouds forever, playing harps in white pajamas. He invites us to relish the thought of a renewed creation and our own renewed bodies as the measure against which we can calculate what suffering with Jesus is worth right now. It is *this* world that will be reborn. It is *our* bodies that will be raised, the way Jesus' body was raised. So we do not have to say good-bye to our bodies in Christian suffering. God will give our bodies back to us – and in better condition, too. I will not be stuck forever with a 50-year old body. My renewed body will be ageless. There is coming a time when you and I will never again ask one another, 'How old are you?' We will not be old. We will never age. And it is *this* body that we care about and *this* world we enjoy that God promises us, all renewed. So we do not have to cling to it now. We can take risks following Jesus. We can lose all things to gain Christ, because, having him, we have all things. We can hold our present possessions with an open hand before God ('those who buy something, as if it were not theirs to keep,' 1 Corinthians 7:30). In the pleasant experiences of this life we sigh, 'Oh, I wish this would last forever,' but it never does. When we enter into our inheritance we will say, 'Oh, I wish this would last forever,' *and it will*.

So living for the Lord, and even paying a price to follow him – we have nothing to lose and everything to inherit! When the gospel comes home to our hearts, we cannot help but be radicalized. This is why God does not aim primarily at our

will-power. He does more than help us grit our teeth and try
to be good. If we get this, really get it, we cannot help but
follow Jesus and consider it a privilege. The promise of glory
has the power to lift a struggling saint out of complacency
and shift him into high gear. If we sense the greatness of the
glory to come, we cannot be typical modern people – grasping,
self-preserving, timid. This gospel confidence makes us more
than conquerors through the One who loved us enough to
buy all of this for us at his own expense and pour it all into
our laps as a gift of grace.

What I respect about Paul is his realism side-by-side with
his hope. Look again at verses 22-23:

> For we know that the whole creation has been groaning together
> in the pains of childbirth until now. And not only the creation,
> but we ourselves, who have the first fruits of the Spirit, groan
> inwardly as we wait eagerly for adoption as sons, the
> redemption of our bodies.

Paul is realistic. The struggles and convulsions in the creation
have been pervasive ever since the curse upon the ground in
the Garden of Eden (Genesis 3:17). Nature is violent,
thrashing about in self-injury. It is 'groaning,' as it were,
because *nobody enjoys dying* – not even the animals. But the
agony of the ages is not meaningless or pointless. Far from
it. The Bible says here that the creation is groaning 'in the
pains of childbirth'. Jesus put it that way too. He said, speaking
of the Endtimes, 'Nation will rise against nation, and kingdom
against kingdom. There will be earthquakes in various places,
and famines. These are the beginning of birth pains' (Mark
13:8, NIV). The disturbances of creation and history signal
the approaching 'birth,' as it were, of a new world governed
by a new human race. This present age of weary longing will
finally be over, and newness will spring forth for us all.

According to verse 23, it is we who have 'the first fruits of the Spirit', the merest beginnings of new life within, whom God has sensitized to the great drama of redemption. We have the Spirit as others do not. That is why we have longings that others hardly feel. We ask questions they do not trouble themselves with. We are bothered by a state of things they have come to accept. They are living for the weekend; we are living for the End, when our very bodies will spring from the grave with immortal vigor. So do not lose your longings! When you groan inwardly and long to be made whole forever, there is nothing wrong with you. When your heart is aching to be rid of sin and frailty, that is not because your Christian life *isn't* working but because it *is* working. Holy restlessness argues life, it argues the presence of the Holy Spirit within you.

What marks a true Christian is an eager, expectant yearning for unseen things. Paul calls it 'hope,' in verses 24-25. The world is satisfied with seen things. They live in hope too, always stretching out for something new, but it is all earthly and present and transient. God is performing a miracle in our hearts. We love this life as much as anyone does, and maybe more, because we know it is the good gift of our Father. (Is there any more delightful sound than the laughter of the saints – deep, rich hilarity bursting from hearts gladdened by the hope of the gospel?) But God is also releasing us from emotional slavery to the passing things of this life (2 Corinthians 4:18). We are not running from life in escapist dreams. By faith we relish a foretaste of eternal things not available now even to Christians. And that is what motivates Christians to press on with rugged endurance – 'patience,' the ESV translates it. We do not panic over the disappointments of this life. We rejoice in the hope of the glory of God (Romans 5:2), because we know it will be worth the wait. We have only begun to see what God can do for us.

So the best is yet to be. The night of sin is almost over for you and me. The dawn is quickly coming. We have 'the first fruits of the Spirit' now, and soon we will also receive 'the redemption of our bodies'. So let's not quit. 'We hope for what we do not see,' but what God has promised. Let's live in expectation. Get up on your tip-toes, as it were, to see what God has in store for you. Think with a biblical imagination about what your future holds. If you will let this future glory capture your heart now, your life will demonstrate the transforming power of gospel hope.

Allan Gardner, missionary to Tierra del Fuego, was sailing to his work there, when the ship had to anchor for the whole winter in a cold and bitter bay. The supply vessel never arrived, and everyone on board his ship, along with Gardner, perished in that desolate place. And yet, the last entry in his journal, written only hours before he died, recorded this: 'This ship is a very Bethel to my soul. I am beyond all power of description happy.' If you open your heart to the power of hope, then your real life, not some ideal life but your real life as it is right now, can be a very Bethel to your soul, such that you become beyond all power of description happy.

Whatever the condition of your heart, look to Jesus. See him there enthroned over all, the Lord of nature and history. See him there, the lover of our souls and even of our bodies. See him there, declaring promises not too trivial for us to believe but so great we struggle to swallow them whole. Look to Jesus. Behold his glory. And whatever the world may say, say with all true Christians, 'Give me Jesus. You can have all this world, but give me Jesus.'

When John Chrysostom, the church father, was brought before the empress Eudoxia, she threatened him with banishment if he insisted upon his Christian independence as a preacher. 'You cannot banish me, for this world is my Father's house.' 'But I will kill you,' said the empress. 'No, you cannot, for my life is hid with Christ in God,' said John.

'I will take away your treasures.' 'No, you cannot, for my treasure is in heaven and my heart is there.' 'But I will drive you away from your friends and you will have no one left.' 'No, you cannot, for I have a friend in heaven from whom you cannot separate me. I defy you, for there is nothing you can do to harm me.'[2]

People whose hearts have laid hold of Christ have a treasure that this world could never give them, a treasure this world can never take away from them. They are transformed people. They are called Christians – ordinary, fun-loving, wholesome, likeable, invincible people. Let's be those Christians here in our generation!

_____

2. Cf. R. Kent Hughes, *Romans* (Wheaton, 1991), page 171. I thank Dr. Tom Nettles for clarifying some of the details of this incident.

Chapter Ten

Too Weak to Pray

[26]Likewise the Spirit helps us in our weakness. For we do not know what to pray for as we ought, but the Spirit himself intercedes for us with groanings too deep for words. [27]And he who searches hearts knows what is the mind of the Spirit, because the Spirit intercedes for the saints according to the will of God.

We come inevitably to those moments in life when nothing will suffice but what is directly and immediately of God.[1] We come to the end of ourselves – no more answers, no more cleverness, *nothing but need*. Even our faith struggles. And there God meets us.

Romans 8:26-27 opens up a neglected insight into the ministry of the Holy Spirit. In verses 1-16, Paul sets before us the work of the Holy Spirit. The Spirit indwells us, translating the finished work of Christ into our personal experience. Then, in verses 17-23, Paul steps back from the ministry of the Spirit to give us a glimpse of what God has in store for us in our future glory. It is so great as to lighten the burden of our present sufferings. According to verses 24-25, we long to experience that glory – the way a young man longs for his wedding day or a prisoner longs for release or a child longs for Christmas morning. That longing, called 'hope', inspires in us patient endurance. Now, in verses 26-27, Paul returns to the work of the Holy Spirit. We have even more than God's promises to motivate us; we also have God's direct help right now. All of Romans 8 argues assurance, certainty. God loves us, and God wants us to *know* that he loves us. The felt love of God produces heroic Christians. And just as the Spirit bears witness to our spirits that we are children of God (verse 16), so 'likewise the Spirit helps us in our weakness' (verse 26) – all for our encouragement.

The word translated *help* is the same one used in Luke 10:40 when Martha was complaining to Jesus about Mary. Martha had been slaving over that hot oven for Jesus, she had set the table with her best china, she was hustling and bustling during the meal, but the task was more than she could cope with. She needed help. She needed Mary to pitch in and bear the burden with her. So Martha said, 'Tell her to *help*

---

1. Cf. H. C. G. Moule, *Romans* (London, 1893), page 232.

me.' That is our word here in verse 26. The Spirit helps us. He undertakes to lighten our load. You and I have a heavy burden to bear. We need a friend to come along and work with us. Why? Because of our 'weakness'.

We are not strong but weak. How are we weak? Well, how *aren't* we weak? Brokenness, unmet needs, emptiness, confusion, weariness, unbelief, fear, dullness, depression, bewilderment, sin – we can be so overwhelmed with the crushing weight of this existence that we do not even know how to pray. The very enormity of our struggles silences us. We do not know what to pray for, as Paul says here. We may be paralyzed in helpless indecision. We may be too distressed to utter a coherent prayer at all. We are weak.

Christians are not always on top of things. Where in the Bible are we taught to expect unruffled composure and unbroken victory? Sometimes life is so troubling, we feel defeated even in prayer. And if we cannot *pray*, we are really in trouble. At that very moment when we most need to draw upon God's promises through prayer – what if we fail at that vital point of connection, when it really counts? Will our weakness bungle the purpose of God? Under normal conditions we tell ourselves that, when all else fails, we can fall back on prayer. But what if we do come to the end of ourselves and our own devices only to discover that we do not even know what to pray, we do not know how to connect the Bible with our experience, and God seems far away? What then? What encouragement can we look to beyond our own radical weakness?

When we are reduced to helplessness, the Holy Spirit will help us. Have you ever thought of the Holy Spirit as a gracious person who steps in to offer, 'May I help? May I bear that burden with you? You're in anguish over your children. You feel forsaken by God. You don't know how to negotiate that important decision. You're lonely. You're tempted. You're sinful. You need to pray. May I help?' The Holy Spirit does not reproach us. He 'gives generously to all without making them feel foolish or guilty' (James 1:5, Phillips).

But *how* does the Holy Spirit help us? Now we enter into deep mystery. The Spirit helps us by interceding for us, Paul explains. When we are too defeated and confused to pray, when the familiar phrases just do not seem adequate any more, when all we can do is groan, the Spirit makes his own appeal on our behalf.

Prayer is more profound than folding our hands and closing our eyes and mouthing well-worn phrases. James Montgomery's hymn has long recognized this:

Prayer is the soul's sincere desire,
unuttered or expressed,
the motion of a hidden fire
that trembles in the breast.

Prayer is the burden of a sigh,
the falling of a tear,
the upward glancing of an eye
when none but God is near.

This too is prayer, both urgent and profound. And it is at moments like this, when the heart moves even beyond words, "the Spirit himself," the Spirit personally and directly, in his immediacy and nearness, helps us by interceding for us "with groanings too deep for words."

Ole Kristian Hallesby (1879-1961) was a Norwegian theologian who stood for biblical truth in an age of doctrinal erosion. He also resisted the Nazi occupation of Norway during World War II and suffered for it in a concentration camp. He understood the depth of prayer. In his book on prayer he wrote this:

I have witnessed the death-struggle of some of my Christian friends. Pain has coursed through their bodies and souls. But this was not their worst experience. I have seen them gaze at me anxiously and ask, "What will become of me when I am no longer able to think a sustained thought, nor pray to God?"

If they only realized what they were doing, the people who postpone conversion until they become ill! My friend, in the death-struggle your physical and mental energies will all be taxed to their utmost by your suffering and pain. Remember that and repent now, the acceptable time.

When I stand at the bedside of friends who are struggling with death, it is blessed to be able to say to them, 'Do not worry about the prayers that you cannot pray. You yourself are a prayer to God at this moment. All that is within you cries out to Him. And He hears all the pleas that your suffering soul and body are making to Him with groanings which cannot be uttered. But if you should have an occasional restful moment, thank God that you already have been reconciled to Him, and that you are now resting in the everlasting arms.'[2]

Verse 26 is the third time we have encountered the word *groan* here in Romans 8. According to verse 22, the whole creation groans. According to verse 23, we groan as we await the redemption of our bodies. But we have the 'first fruits of the Spirit'. So we know that God has more for us. We look to him during our sighs and tears and doubts. And the Spirit translates our struggles into his own intercession 'with groanings too deep for words'.

Do you realize that, if you are in Christ, the Holy Spirit indwells you in such a way that your spirit is united with God's Spirit? This union does not make you perfect. But God's Spirit does manifest his will, his mind, his affections through your own spirit and heart and inner being – the you

---

2. O. Hallesby, *Prayer* (Minneapolis, 1944 reprint), pages 148-149.

inside that is really you. In Galatians 4:6 Paul writes that, because we are God's children, God has sent the Spirit into our hearts crying, 'Abba, Father!' Now think about that. God has sent the Holy Spirit into our hearts. And what does the Holy Spirit do inside us? He cries, 'Abba, Father!' But is God the Father of the Spirit? No, Paul's whole point is that God is *our* Father. It is *our* hearts that cry, 'Abba, Father!' But our hearts have been so indwelt by the Holy Spirit that *the Spirit* inspires that cry in *our* hearts. As far as prayer is concerned, there is a profound union of our spirits with God's Spirit.

So in verse 23, we groan. In verse 26, the Spirit groans – through our own struggles in prayer. He is *in* our struggles, directing our faith to God, not letting our faith die, helping our hope to persevere. He is lifting, through our wordless yearnings, prayers that he himself translates into the wisdom of heaven.

We still agonize. And sometimes we may teeter on the very edge of the abyss. But why is it that our hearts still lay hold of God and refuse to let go? The Holy Spirit is helping us. He creates in us a rugged insistence that our God is a mighty fortress. He deepens our faith with fresh insight into God's promises. He shows us how desperate our need for God really is. He stirs up God-ward desires and prompts in us frequent, if inarticulate, visits to the throne of grace.[3]

And, according to verse 27, the Father discerns within our heavy-hearted yearnings the clear mind, the godly intention, the winning voice of the Holy Spirit. In searching the sighs of our hearts, God finds the Spirit. And Paul's point in the second half of verse 27 is that this helping ministry of the Spirit is God's will for the saints.

---

3. Cf. John Owen, 'A Discourse Concerning the Holy Spirit,' in *The Works of John Owen* (Edinburgh, 1981 reprint), III:398-399.

So if all you can do is lift your heart-cry to God, that does not prove that you are not a saint. Just the opposite. This is God's way with 'the saints'. It is hypocrites who always have the answers and always have something to say and think they know everything. But it is the saints who are led by the Spirit (verse 14) out into the extremities of life, where all they have left is empty hands lifted before God, all they have left is the anguish of their hearts, all they have left is *nothing but need* – it is helpless people like that whom the Holy Spirit helps to lay hold of God, even more than they know. Such believers are not failing to live the victorious life. They are, in fact, more than conquerors, even when they do not even know what to pray. They are God's saints, living out his plan not only in its glorious outcome but even in its agonizing process.

How amazing that God perfects his strength in our weakness, even in prayer! Thank God for the indwelling Holy Spirit! Thank God for the intimacy and nearness and readiness of the Holy Spirit! Thank God that our future does not stand or fall on the brilliance of our praying but on the all-sufficiency of God!

Now what lessons can we draw from these verses about our life with God? First, the Christian life is not getting saved and then doing the best you can after that. From beginning to end, the Christian life is God's power made perfect in our weakness. We never graduate out of weakness, even in prayer. And if that is so, then we can admit how weak we really are, even in prayer. The authentic Christian life is not people who always know what to do and how to pray but simply people who have the Holy Spirit helping them in their weakness.

Secondly, do not expect God to wait until you have enough understanding before he stretches you – even beyond the range of your capacity to pray. He will take you out beyond comfortable understanding. He will take you to the point that you say, 'Where is God in *this*?' And the answer – or, better, the assurance – is that he is right there with you in your suffering. Indeed, he dwells within you, the sufferer, lifting your ignorance and frustration out of futility through the Holy Spirit. God will take you beyond what you can explain and cope with and say to you, 'Even here I meet you and help you and turn your defeat into my triumph.' God will show you and me that we do not live by explanations and coping devices; we live by faith. God himself, God alone, is our all-sufficient salvation. The Christian life is not God out there and our methods down here within our reach. God is our refuge and strength right here, right now. And he will take every one of us where he took Job, who eventually said, 'My ears had heard of you, but now my eyes have seen you' (Job 42:5). God will take us down deep enough into life, until we really feel that 'underneath are the everlasting arms' (Deuteronomy 33:27). And as the Lord leads us along, our theology may tend to simplify as it matures. More and more, we may find ourselves saying, 'There's a lot I don't understand. But I do know *God*. I trust *him*.' Our hearts will exult to say with the psalmist, 'Our God is in the heavens; he does whatever he pleases' (Psalm 115:3).

Thirdly, do not worry about finding the 'right' words to pray meaningfully to God. If you find in your heart a longing for God's salvation, his help, his will, his nearness, his glory, then your prayer need be nothing more than a sigh. Can you groan? I hope so. God's saints are not superficial people. They groan. They groan with the assurance that a groan is all they need to get through to God. A yearning, a heart-cry – that is enough for God. So do not lose your longings. The Holy Spirit is in those longings. If you did have all the answers, you would not yearn as deeply. And that would not be success. Feelings of human adequacy are defeat; feelings of human inadequacy are that point of breakthrough into divine power. Do not think that longings are an immature phase you should grow out of. Your godly longings are profound. Isn't it true that our best moments with the Lord are when our hearts, broken with our own need, littleness and mess, are melted into longings for him and his glory?

When the only prayer you can manage is a groan, that is a beautiful prayer in the sight of God. It is humanly weak, but it has power in heaven through the Holy Spirit. When your heart utters that simple cry, the Holy Spirit is taking you to a new depth of yieldedness. You do not have to know what to do next. You only need to cling to God. Maybe for some of us, the greatest thing that could happen is not some new doctrinal insight, valuable as that is, but a new breakthrough in our hearts, new longings for God, new sighs and groans.

You do not need to pretend that you are a better Christian than you really are. God does not need your success; he searches your weakness for the mind of the Spirit. If all you have is a longing for God's will and glory, he will see to it that you *get* God's will in all things (verse 28). So go to God just as you are. You need not bear your burden one moment longer. Cast all your care on him, for he cares for you (1 Peter 5:7).

Fourthly, your Father not only knows you, he understands you. We do not understand ourselves, much less one another, in the afflictions of life. But we do not need to understand in order to pray, because God does understand. And he is able to deploy our gasps and sighs for his mighty purposes. The faintest whisper of your heart is fully known to God and fully useful to God. And when you lie in a hospital bed with tubes stuck into you and you can hardly put two sentences together, the Spirit will intercede for you through your groans. And when you have a stroke and cannot speak properly and you find yourself cut off even from those who love you most and all you have left is a desire to go home to be with the Lord, he will hear the longings of your heart. And when you are hit by a drunk driver and your life-blood is flowing out of you in the twisted wreckage of your car, in those final moments of semi-consciousness, when all you can do is moan, God will understand your prayer, take your devastation into his mighty hands and subdue it to his glorious purpose.

Finally, prayer is not changing God's mind. Prayer is our brokenness, longing for nothing but the will and glory of God. When his will is all we have left – no clever answers, no human remedies, no pride, nothing but need – there the Holy Spirit enters in. To be humbled into the dust, when all we have left is a longing for God, what a breakthrough! To be reduced to yearning, so that he alone is our all in all, what cleansing! That is how revival could come. May God accelerate his Spirit's work among us.

Chapter Eleven

All Things for Good?

[28]And we know that for those who love God all things work together for good, for those who are called according to his purpose.

Gambling is big these days, sadly. But the lottery is more than a game. It is a way of looking at life. If you cannot get ahead through working and planning and brains, why not through chance? Life is chance, isn't it? Isn't the lottery just a parable of the way life works? Isn't life just a matter of luck, of being in the right place at the right time – or the wrong place, for that matter?

Other people feel that their lives are not by chance at all, but are very much under the control of some cosmic Fate. They think that the planets guide their fortunes. So they read the horoscopes to see what Jupiter is going to do to them next. But if you believe in Fate, you have no reason for taking initiative. There is a demoralizing inevitability in Fate. You just give up, and what will be will be.

But the Bible teaches us another way of seeing our lives. The hand of God is at the helm. He is steering us through the storms of life toward home, toward a safe haven. And he takes care to order all the events of our lives right now to speed us on our way there. This is what we call Providence – God's overruling hand at work everywhere in a fallen world. The Providence of God is 'the underlying premise of everything that is taught in the Scriptures.'[1] The biblical confidence in the Providence of God is a faith so bold, so demanding, so unapologetic, that we cannot believe it half-way. Either all things work together for our good, or *nothing* makes sense. We must be either transformed Christians or bitter skeptics, because we cannot just *sort of* believe Romans 8:28. We either believe it or we doubt it. There is no middle ground.

A personal confidence in God's providential love in all things, including bad things, is powerful. It makes a

1. Cf. 'Providence,' in *The Evangelical Dictionary of Biblical Theology*, edited by Walter A. Elwell (Grand Rapids, 1996), page 650.

difference. In the early 1740s a ship was sailing from England to Georgia. On board were twenty-six German Moravian missionaries – men, women and children. During their journey across the Atlantic, as they were holding a worship service, a storm broke out. The English passengers screamed in panic. But these Christians looked up and calmly sang on. An English passenger later asked, 'Were you not afraid?' 'I thank God, no,' said one of the Christians. 'But were not your women and children afraid?' 'No; our women and children are not afraid to die.' That astonished Englishman was a man named John Wesley. And those Christians, demonstrating the transforming power of the gospel in the middle of a storm, were instrumental in the conversion of one of history's great evangelists.[2] All around us every day are potential evangelists and scholars and pastors and missionaries and social reformers and writers and doctors and influential Christians of all sorts. We know them right now as our non-Christian friends. And God has positioned us in the midst of our storms to show them the practical difference that Jesus makes.

What would our lives look like, if we feared nothing but God? What difference would it make if we no longer feared truth, the cost of discipleship, repentance, change, the future? What difference would it make if we fixed our desires not on popularity and money and predictability and control but on being conformed to the image of God's Son? What do fearless people look like? They look like German Moravian missionaries on a little wooden ship in the middle of the Atlantic when a storm threatens to drown them all and they calmly sing on because they believe in the providential love of God. And when people like that appear here in this fearful world, they make Jesus an unavoidable issue to others.

---

2. Cf. A. Skevington Wood, *The Inextinguishable Blaze* (Grand Rapids, 1960), pages 105f.

Fearless people are influential people. They stand out. They are convincing. Down deep in your heart, wouldn't you love to be unleashed to live boldly for the Lord? Wouldn't you love to be intimidated no longer, but upright and courageous for God? Wouldn't it be satisfying to live right out loud? Let the whole world see the difference that Romans 8:28 makes in the lives of normal, real, life-affirming people! And may we draw *many* John Wesleys to Christ as we live out the courage of Romans 8:28!

Like those Moravian missionaries on that ship, we are not afraid of anything, because we know that in all things God works for the good of those who love him, who have been called according to his purpose.

Romans 8:28 begins with a contrast. 'And we know' contrasts with 'we do not know' of verse 26. There is so much we do not know and do not understand in life. We do not know (verse 26), we know (verse 28) – that's a summary of authentic Christianity. We must never assert anything beyond the range of what we really know. We must never hold back in timidity from affirming what we do know.

So amid the perplexities of life, what *do* we know? We know this: For those who love God all things work together for good, for those who are called according to his purpose. And this one thing we know breaks down into four parts.

First, we know that '*all things*'. Not some things, not most things, not the nice things, but all things – including evil and tragedy. Ever since Adam fell into sin, God has been taking our sorrows and even our failures and bending them around to serve his own loving intentions. You are at this moment enveloped in the love of God as in an atmosphere, and nothing can touch you without his gracious and wise permission. I will not hesitate to say that even our sins fall within the scope of 'all things'. This can be misunderstood, but how could it be otherwise? Can I sin my way out of the saving purpose of

God? I can easily sin my way out of a clear conscience, out of the assurance of my salvation, out of my ministry, out of my marriage, my children's respect, financial solvency, a good reputation, my health. I can easily sin my way into disgrace and heartache and a sexually transmitted disease and bankruptcy and mediocrity and tragic inconsequentiality. But I cannot sin my way out of the purpose of God, because my sin is the very thing his saving purpose most intentionally redeems. 'All things' must extend to literally all things in our lives, or else Romans 8:28 loses its force. If there is even one single experience of life falling outside the range of 'all things', then we can never rest assured that God's love employs the worst of life for his loving purpose. But if 'all things' means literally *all* things, then we need never wonder, 'Is this the moment when God is abandoning me? Have I just stepped outside the scope of his power and his claims and his resources and his care?'

But make no mistake. The boldness of Romans 8:28 does not condone our sins. It does not soften the hard consequences of our sins. It does not give us an excuse to look the other way in denial. God is able to use our sins to sting us into repentance. But that only illustrates the truth of Romans 8:28. *Nothing* can outmaneuver the mercy of God for us, if God intends mercy for us.

Your hang-up right now, seen through the lens of Romans 8:28, invites you into a new beginning with God. Paul Tournier offers this perspective:

> The most wonderful thing in this world is not the good that we accomplish, but the fact that good can come out of the evil that we do. . . . Our vocation is, I believe, to build good out of evil. For if we try to build good out of good, we are in danger of running out of raw material.[3]

---

3. Cf. Philip Yancey, 'Chess Master,' *Christianity Today*, 22 May 2000, page 112.

That is a realistic assessment of the task of life. But even more wonderfully than the good we can build out of evil, the burden of Romans 8:28 is the good *God* is building out of *all* things, including evil. Isn't it wonderful to realize that we live in a universe run by a God like this? This is assurance enough to set our hearts singing again. Our lives right now, as they are, are the raw material of God's good work.

Secondly, we know that 'all things *work*'. On this very day God is going about unseen in your life and mine, moving his loving purpose forward in a thousand different ways. He is even at work for us when others are at work against us. In Genesis 50:20 Joseph says to his treacherous brothers, 'You meant it for evil, but God meant it for good.' They had betrayed him and sold him into slavery. They meant Joseph harm. But God was also at work in that experience. With prophetic insight, Joseph sees that two intentions can guide a single event – a human intention ('you meant it') and a divine intention ('but God meant it'). And we can say more. It is possible not only for two intentions to bring about one event, but it is also possible for those two intentions to be morally antithetical. 'You meant it *for evil*, but God meant it *for good.*' Both evil and good can be intended at two levels of causation activating one single event. The purpose of Joseph's brothers was murderous, but the purpose of God in that same event was life-giving. And God's purpose overruled their purpose. God bent the evil human act around toward a beautiful divine outcome. And here in Romans 8:28, Paul's point is that God works this way in *all* things, even when evil is involved. Life does not fall out this way just now and then but all the time. God's goodness is both pervasive and invincible. Life is not chance and luck. God is at work.

Moreover, 'all things work *together*'. So much in life looks like a random mess, doesn't it? Where is the pattern to it all? How does one experience relate to another? We wonder about this especially when something in our past that cannot be changed conspires today to hold us back. But Romans 8:28 is making the astonishing claim that God is at work behind the scenes in all things, overruling the devil's malice and our own folly, so that the various experiences of our lives *coordinate together* to advance God's loving purpose. He carefully joins one moment with another, however distant, so that his plan succeeds. Doesn't this assurance moderate the bitterness of our regrets?

Thirdly, we know that 'all things work together *for good*'. How could it be otherwise? God *is* good. To say that God works for our good is only another way of saying that God is God. Goodness is so essential to his nature and ways that you can point to the truth of Romans 8:28 and say, in effect, '*This is God.*'

Romans 8:28 does not say that all things *are* good. Cancer is not good but evil. Injustice is not good but evil. Sin is not good but evil. We should never lie down before evil and acquiesce. We should always oppose evil. But sometimes God overrules our opposition and allows evil to triumph over us. And when he does, our part is to trust him to take even this dark thread of evil and weave it into his larger tapestry of glorious good.

So what *is* that 'good' toward which all things are working together? That 'good' is not to make us rich or popular or healthy or successful. God might give us some of these things. But God has not promised us such things in this life. They are expendable. The 'good' to which God is *committed* appears right here in verse 29: 'conformed to the image of his Son.' And there it is again in verse 30: 'those whom he justified he also glorified.' That is the 'good' God is striving after in our lives – to make us glorious like his Son.

And this is where language fails us. The word *good* understates the value of God's care for us. If you were an artist and you showed me your *magnum opus*, that one work that brings you the most satisfaction because it so beautifully expresses what's most meaningful to you, and if I looked at it and said, 'That's good,' would you be happy? But here in Romans 8:28, what is the word *good* worth? It is worth this: being changed from what we are right now, with all our struggles and failures, and being liberated into the glorious image of God's Son in resurrection immortality forever. Not bad.

Do you realize that, if you are in Christ, you are God's personal project? He has undertaken to make you glorious. So if this is what God values for you, let this be what you value for yourself and those you love. Let your heart embrace as good what God's heart embraces as good. Let nothing in your heart resist the work of God in you. Rejoice in your hope of the glory of God (Romans 5:2). Set your heart on being made like Christ, and do not set your heart on the expendable things of this life. If you invest your affections wisely, if your emotional commitments line up with God's emotional commitments, your happiness becomes invincible.

The fourth and last part of what we know here is that 'all things work together for good' – for whom? '*for those who love God . . . for those who are called according to his purpose.*' Romans 8:28 does not belong to everyone alike. It belongs only to those who can be described in these two ways.

From the human perspective, the people who own Romans 8:28 love God. They do not just believe the Bible, important as that is. They do not just go to church, important as that is. They love God. They embrace his purpose. They are no longer happy in sin. They want what pleases God. They gladly suffer the loss of all things, in order to gain Christ. People who love God – they are the ones to whom the assurance of Romans 8:28 belongs. And this is right, because the mentality of love is all-inclusive. Love entails trust and hope and all the other virtues of the heart that bind us to God. And love for God is most convincing when offered to him in the furnace of affliction. Love does not resent God. It does not rage against God. Love bows in worship and accepts the will of God with expectation of good.

Isn't it remarkable that when Paul identifies those for whom God thinks and plans and labors, he considers their heart-level *relationship* with God? They are people who *love* God. Does that describe you? Do you love him? Correct opinions, church membership and faithful service all have their place, but do you love God? Do you understand how important it is to *God* that you love him? Do you understand how important it is for *you* that you love him? Jesus said, 'Anyone who loves his father or mother more than me is not worthy of me; anyone who loves his son or daughter more than me is not worthy of me' (Matthew 10:37, NIV). Paul wrote, 'If anyone does not love the Lord – a curse be on him' (1 Corinthians 16:22). And elsewhere Paul wrote, 'Grace to all who love our Lord Jesus Christ with love undying' (Ephesians 6:24). What could be more encouraging to us than that people would look at us and say with wonder, 'How they love God!'

From the divine perspective, those who love God do so because they have been called according to God's purpose. They love him, because he first loved them (1 John 4:19). They have found the call of the gospel to be not just an invitation but a summons. They have not just been invited but brought in. The called look at themselves with wonder at the transformation God is effecting and they have to say, 'I am what I am by the grace of God' (1 Corinthians 15:10). 'I am amazed at myself. I am no longer the person I once was. Look at what God is doing!'

Have you been called? Are you amazed at yourself? Has your life been interrupted and redirected by the personal call of God to your heart? Those whom God calls come under personal conviction of sin. They feel their helplessness. They are drawn to Jesus as their only Savior, and they run to him. And, when God finds them, they are not even looking to get saved. They are indifferent. They are distracted. They are like everybody else. But then God approaches them and calls them, and they change. They come alive to God. Has God called you? Do you find a growing fearlessness within yourself, in keeping with Romans 8:28? Are you experiencing the transforming power of the gospel? Can you say from the Holy Spirit's work in your heart that nothing will ever separate you from the love of God in Christ Jesus our Lord? Is that a strong assurance in your heart or just words on the page? If there is any uncertainty in your mind, set lesser things aside and seek the Lord while he may be found. Call upon him while he is near. Forsake your sins and turn to the Lord. He will deal with you mercifully and freely pardon you and lead you into these great certainties as your own personal possession.[4]

---

4. Cf. D. M. Lloyd-Jones, *Romans: An Exposition of Chapter 8:17-39, The Final Perseverance of the Saints* (Edinburgh, 1998 reprint), pages 190-194.

Chapter Twelve

The Unbroken Chain

[29] For those whom he foreknew he also predestined to be conformed to the image of his Son, in order that he might be the firstborn among many brothers. [30] And those whom he predestined he also called, and those whom he called he also justified, and those whom he justified he also glorified.

Years ago when we lived in Scotland, I traveled with a friend from our village near Aberdeen to the town of Oban on the west coast. As we drove around town, my friend pointed out a circular, stone building, sort of like a small Roman coliseum, on a hill overlooking Oban. He explained to me that this building is called 'McCaig's Folly.' Mr. McCaig was a banker in town who built this structure in the late nineteenth century. But it is called 'McCaig's *Folly*' because it was never completed. To this day, that unfinished building stands as an embarrassing reminder of one man's lack of foresight and resources. But God builds no follies. The work God begins in us, he completes.

If our redemption could be compared to a building project, we could say this. The plans were drawn up in eternity past. The price was paid in advance, in full, by Christ at his cross. The foundation was laid in our conversion. We are now under construction. And God builds no follies.

Romans 8 affirms that what God has begun in us, he will complete. All things work together for our good by thrusting us forward into more of the love of God. That means that nothing can ever separate us from the love of God in Christ Jesus our Lord. And what is this love of God, but his work of redemption in our lives? Nothing can ever deprive us of our full joy in God's eternal presence, for God builds no follies.

Life often feels like defeat, doesn't it? So Paul wants us to feel something else. It is as if Paul invites us to bend down with him and touch with our hands the bedrock underneath us – the absolute certainty of God's eternal love toward us – and not only to touch it but to stamp on it with our feet to feel its absolute solidity, so that we become convinced that nothing will ever separate us from the love of God in Christ Jesus our Lord. The logical outcome of Romans 8 is that we feel no hesitation about where we stand with God and the thrilling certainty of his love.

Coming out of verse 28, Paul is answering several questions at once: *Why* do all things work together for our good? What *is* that good toward which all things are working together? What is God's 'purpose', according to which we have been called? Verse 28 is so sweeping in its claim that Paul now puts it within a larger framework so that we are all the more persuaded and emboldened.

New Testament Christianity has the power to create personal greatness in us. It is a renewing force unleashed into a human life with transforming effect. The courage of the early church burned on the high octane fuel of Romans 8. Paul did not write this to the Roman church so that they could discuss it in the abstract. He wrote Romans 8 so that the Christians in Rome could walk into the arenas and face the lions with songs of praise on their lips because they felt in their hearts more keenly than they felt the lions' fangs in their throats that nothing could ever separate them from the love of God. The gospel has always been a transforming power and it always will be, when by God's grace we make it our own personal possession.

It is one thing to believe that God's plan cannot fail. It is another thing to know that you yourself *are* God's loving, invincible plan – you, deployed by God himself in history to demonstrate before men and angels the transforming power of the gospel – you, a living sacrifice willingly aflame on the altar of God's mercy. When that kind of personal certainty lays hold of our hearts, expelling all hesitation, that is when we rise up with heroic greatness. So we come to verses 29-30 to learn from our mentor, the apostle Paul, how to live and how to die in the atmosphere of a blazing certainty that God loves us with an endless love.

These verses are marked by five great verbs – foreknew, predestined, called, justified and glorified – five mountain peaks in the landscape of God's eternal plan to take us from guilt to glory. The logical coherence of these two verses, marked by these five verbs, forms an unbroken chain of God's loving intentions for his own.

First, 'For those whom he *foreknew.*' We must not misunderstand what Paul means by this word *foreknew*. He is not saying that in eternity past God looked down through the corridor of time and foresaw who would trust him and follow him, and it was these whom God predestined. Paul cannot mean that. He cannot mean that God's foreknowledge was mere foresight, because God foresaw every human being who would exist. But he did not predestine everyone to be conformed to the image of his Son. Not everybody ends up in heaven. So God's foreknowledge here must be more than mere foresight, because foreknowledge translates into predestination ('those whom he foreknew he also predestined'). What does it mean that God 'foreknew' us?

One of the ways the Bible describes God's care for us is to say that he 'knows' us. For example, 'The Lord *knows* the way of the righteous, but the way of the wicked will perish' (Psalm 1:6). In fact, the New International Version paraphrases that verse: 'The Lord *watches over* the way of the righteous.' Why does the NIV interpret 'knows' as 'watches over'? Because, in the sense of mere awareness, God knows both the way of the righteous and the way of the wicked. So God's knowledge of the righteous must be more than awareness. It is love, his 'watching over'. In Amos 3:2 God says to Israel, 'You only have I *known* out of all the families of the earth.' But again, God knows all the nations of the earth. So the NIV paraphrases: 'You only have I *chosen* of all the families of the earth.' God 'knows' his own in a special way. Here in Romans 8 Paul is using this biblical language to describe God's devoted attention to us and his loving choice of us.

Paul adds a prefix 'fore-' to 'know' ('whom he *fore*knew')

to signal that God knew us and cared about us *before* we knew him or cared about him – in fact, before we even existed in time. Amazingly, God set his love on us before time began: 'God chose us in Christ before the creation of the world' (Ephesians 1:4).

The point is that God initiated our relationship with him. God made the first move toward us. He did not wait for us to show any interest in him. God was not just stuck with us. He *chose* us. He did not have to make do with the likes of us. He *chose* us. Therefore, your place in God's love is secured not by what you have done for him but by his own infinite capacity to love sin-infested, God-hating, foot-dragging sinners. This is why our fundamental response to God will always be a kind of wondering trust: 'What am *I* doing here? Why does God love *me*? What infinite resources of love must resonate within the being of God!'

Secondly, 'For those whom he foreknew he also *predestined*.' Again, the prefix ('he also *pre*destined') locates God's loving initiative in eternity past, when he predetermined our final destination. That is pre-destination – he *pre*-determined our final *destination* in heaven. He not only saw us thrashing about in our blasphemy and misery and self-injury and set his love on us, but also he resolved, 'I will not leave them as they are. I will put honor upon them. I will bring them to glory. I will conform them to the image of my own Son. I will highlight his supremacy by exalting their dignity.' God resolved long ago that *many* restored sinners would live eternally in heaven, surrounding Jesus Christ, reflecting his glory, all radiant with resurrection immortality ('conformed to the image of his Son').

So this is how we should think of predestination. Predestination is not a fire insurance policy to keep sleepy semi-believers out of hell with their complacent sins undisturbed. Predestination is God's purpose to make us like

Christ and to fit us to be forever with Christ. If you are not pursuing God's purpose that you would be holy and blameless in his sight (Ephesians 1:4), then predestination is not yours. Predestination is not a bed of ease for sinful self-indulgence; it is an encouragement for personal transformation. Let's pursue what God has planned – that we would be conformed to the image of God's Son. If we will, we will find all of God's love supporting our pursuit.

Thirdly, everyone whom God foreknew and predestined he has called: 'And those whom he predestined he also *called*.' There is no 'fore-' or 'pre-' prefix to this verb, because Paul is describing our actual experience of things in the here and now. His sweep of thought moves from the heart of God in eternity past to the action of God in our present lives. When God calls us through the Spirit-empowered gospel, we convert to faith in Jesus. He gives us the faith to respond. If you have put your trust in Christ, it may have felt as though you were reaching out to find God. You may have struggled to take that step. But Paul sees beyond your choice of God. He is explaining what lay beneath your heartcry to God – *God* was calling *you*. The anonymous hymn-writer put it this way:

> I sought the Lord and afterward I knew
> he moved my soul to seek him, seeking me;
> it was not I that found, O Savior true;
> no, I was found of thee.

How else can we explain the fact that we self-excusing, evasive sinners finally admitted, 'Everything in my whole life has been skewed. I've been wrong all along. God is better qualified to run my life and prepare my eternity than I am'? How does the self-flattering human heart come to that admission? There we were, just ordinary, well-meaning, self-admiring sinners on our way to hell. But God had other plans. He set his love on us. He determined that we would be glorified. He arranged that you and he, personally, would meet. He drew near to you through the gospel. He spoke to your heart. You heard his call and woke up. This is why predestination and evangelism are compatible. God translated his eternal purpose into your actual experience by calling you through the gospel.

Fourthly, 'and those whom he called he also *justified.*' Why did God do that? Because the people he loves are *sinners.* The people God works with have wrecked their relationship with him. But God refuses to accept their destructive failure as the last word. God says, '*Whatever it takes*, I will restore them to my favor. My love is willing to pay the price.' So God 'made him who knew no sin to be sin on our behalf, that we might become the righteousness of God in him' (2 Corinthians 5:21, NASB). When our real moral guilt is written off and we are judged righteous through Jesus' merit, he is honored. And that is God's plan – that Jesus Christ would be 'the firstborn,' the honored one among us (verse 29). It is all 'for the sake of his name' (Romans 1:5).

Isn't it interesting that Paul does not even mention our faith here? We are justified by faith (Romans 5:1). Paul argued strongly for that truth earlier in this letter (3:21-4:25). So why does he choose not to mention our faith here? He wants us to see wave after wave of God's loving initiative washing over us, and drawing attention to our faith here might obscure our vision of God. Our faith does not justify us; God does. It is all of God. Faith does not qualify us for justification. Faith is merely the empty hand receiving the gift of justification. We must look beyond our faith to God. An unselfconscious focus on God himself *is* faith.

Finally, 'those whom he justified he also *glorified.*' We are looking here at God's plan. And his plan directs our gaze into the future, when we will be glorified in heaven – like Christ, with Christ. No more lying awake at night wrestling with thoughts of self-reproach. No more haunting memories of shame and remorse. No more fear of discipline and exposure, because *no more sin*! The blood of Jesus will rinse us completely clean and we will stand before God as personal, individual reflections of the perfection of Christ. Our final redemption is called 'glorification', because sin is not just bad; it is humiliating. Jesus did not die just to make us good; he died to make us great and glorious and conformed to the image of God's Son.

But if we will not be glorified until we get to heaven, why does Paul put this verb in the past tense ('glorified')? Paul moves with one giant step from our justification all the way through the struggles of this life to our glorification in heaven. Why does he look beyond what is so painfully obvious to us right now? Because the connection between our justification and our glorification is unbreakable. In fact, everyone whom God foreknew and predestined and called and justified he also glorified. Look at the structure and logic of Paul's very grammar here. The objects of the verbs 'foreknew' and 'predestined' and 'called' and 'justified' and 'glorified' are all the same people. No one falls through the cracks along the way. The people God starts out with are the same ones he ends up with. This is God's loving plan. And that is the point. Paul is showing us what God has planned, not necessarily what we have experienced yet. He spreads the blueprint out before us on the table and describes it from start to finish as one complete act of God – a *fait accompli*. And that is why Paul puts the verb *glorify* in the past tense. The purpose of God is *that* certain. The cross of Jesus is *that* powerful. The love of the Father is *that* resourceful and persistent. God loves us with *that* kind of love. And *that* is the bedrock we stand on.

So Paul scans the sweep of God's loving purpose from eternity past, through time, into eternity future, and he reasons this way: If God is guiding his eternal plan for our glory (verses 29-30), then he must be guiding our present experience for our good (verse 28). Your life is only a thin slice of time within the entire length of history. Time itself is just a brief parenthesis within the vast field of eternity. God's plan spans all of time, from eternity to eternity. His loving plan achieves our glorious, Christlike good. Therefore, God must be overseeing our brief pilgrimage now for our good. Should we not trust him and think well of him and follow him through anything to get there?

Behold the glory of the Lord! See his power to transform sinners into reflections of Jesus Christ. See the sheer massiveness of his eternality, as he dwells outside time, equally present to all points of time at once, guiding your future toward your glory when you cannot even see it yet. See the ease with which he triumphs over your enemies, the world, the flesh, the devil, who are not even mentioned here. God alone is the subject of all these verbs. He stands forth as himself our sole and sufficient guarantee of eternal glory. We see our enemies in verses 31-39, but none here when Paul spreads out God's loving plan. Why? Because God himself is all we need. If *God* is for us, who can be against us? Behold the glory of the Lord! Esteem him. Worship him. Value him. Jonathan Edwards said, 'As to gold, silver and diamonds, earthly crowns and kingdoms, God often throws them out to those whom he esteems as dogs and swine.' But transforming grace is 'the peculiar gift of God which he bestows only on his special favorites.' It is 'the special benefit which Christ died to procure for his elect, the most excellent token of his everlasting love; the chief fruit of his great labors, and the most precious purchase of his blood.'[1] If God has

---

1. Jonathan Edwards, 'True Grace Distinguished from the Experience of Devils,' in *The Works of Jonathan Edwards* (Edinburgh, 1979 reprint), II:50.

included you in his loving plan, how rich you are, whatever else you may lack! If you have rejected God's loving purpose, how poor you are, whatever else you may own!

What more does God have to do? His gospel is calculated to bring us to such finality that our hearts cry out, 'Okay, that's it. No more doubts for me. God loves me. The blood of his Son is cleansing me. His Spirit is living within me. That's how committed God is to me – and not just to the church in general but to me personally. You know, I think everything's going to be all right. No more hesitation! No more uncertainty! Come what may in this present evil age, I belong to God. So, Lord, let me live fully for you now. Let me live before I die!' Will you say that to God? If not, why not? Again, what more does God have to do until you live boldly for his glory? If Romans 8 cannot convince you, what will? If Romans 8 cannot light your fire, then you have a problem, because God has nothing greater to say – no greater promises, no greater atonement, no greater indwelling, no greater love. Will you say to God, 'Lead me into heroic, sin-expelling, world-conquering, authentic Christianity. Let me, even me, demonstrate the transforming power of the gospel'?

Chapter Thirteen

Love Unending

[31]What then shall we say to these things? If God is for us, who can be against us? [32]He who did not spare his own Son but gave him up for us all, how will he not also with him graciously give us all things? [33]Who shall bring any charge against God's elect? It is God who justifies. [34]Who is to condemn? Christ Jesus is the one who died – more than that, who was raised – who is at the right hand of God, who indeed is interceding for us. [35]Who shall separate us from the love of Christ? Shall tribulation, or distress, or persecution, or famine, or nakedness, or danger, or sword? [36]As it is written, 'For your sake we are being killed all the day long; we are regarded as sheep to be slaughtered.' [37]But in all these things we are more than conquerors through him who loved us. [38]For I am sure that neither death nor life, nor angels nor rulers, nor things present nor things to come, nor powers, [39]nor height nor depth, nor anything else in all creation, will be able to separate us from the love of God in Christ Jesus our Lord.

God wants us to feel loved. If we feel condemned and abandoned, we become vulnerable to the seductions coming at us from all sides. But God wants us to feel loved – not with sentimentality but with a deep *certainty* that God Almighty in heaven is not opposed to us, though we deserve it; he is *for* us. God is doing something good with our lives. We are moving in a positive direction, and nothing can deflect us from that course. If we did not qualify for God's love to begin with, how can we disqualify ourselves now?

A strong confidence in God's loving intentions and enveloping care fortifies us to face whatever life throws at us. Richard Sibbes, the Puritan pastor, put it beautifully:

> God takes care of poor weak Christians that are struggling with temptations and corruptions. Christ carries them in his arms. All Christ's sheep are diseased, and therefore he will have a tender care of them.[2]

Our certainty does not lie in our apprehension of God's grace but in his grace itself. It is the very objectivity of God's love that is so satisfying and meets our need for absolute assurance. As we walk through this world, we are a target. The world, the flesh and the devil are determined to prevent our safe arrival in heaven, or at least to harass us on our way there. But we will defy them, because God is for us. He is on our side.

We have seen in Romans 8 that there is now no condemnation against us, sinners that we are, because God has united us with Christ. We have seen that the Holy Spirit indwells us. He marks us as people with a new, spiritual mentality. We have seen that the Spirit takes away our dread of God and draws our hearts up to God with a new sense of

---

1. 'Divine Meditations,' in *The Works of Richard Sibbes* (Edinburgh, 1982 reprint), VII:185.

his fatherly goodness. We have seen that the built-in processes of the whole creation will someday be released into their true powers when we, God's children, inherit the glories of our redemption. We have seen that, as we make our difficult way through the pilgrimage of this life, God is always at work for our good, conforming us to the image of his Son. And the loving purpose of God will infallibly bring us into our eternal glorification.

So at this point Paul cannot restrain himself any longer. 'What then shall we say to these things?' erupts from his heart, and then he goes about answering that question by asking more questions in the rest of the passage. Isn't that suggestive in itself? Rather than protect a vulnerable gospel from hard, embarrassing questions, he invites us to think daringly, outwardly, expansively. So what is the gospel worth to us? What is its practical cash value? How much pounding can it take and still hold together? 'Let's think,' Paul says. 'Let's think boldly. I am not ashamed of the gospel.' He had thought it through for himself, and he knew that the gospel, and only the gospel, stands up to the tests of real life. Paul shows us how, in verses 31-39, by asking four powerful questions.[3]

First, in verse 31, Paul asks, 'If God is for us, who can be against us?' Paul does not simply ask, 'Who is against us?' We can think of many who are against us. Our own evil hearts are against us. The devil is against us. This present evil age is against us. And trying to remain true to Christ, armed with our puny virtue, is like going up against a tank battalion with a pea shooter. We are defeated already.

So Paul does not ask the question that way. He asks, '*If*

---

2. Cf. John R. W. Stott, *Men Made New* (Downers Grove, 1976), pages 103-106. Stott interprets Paul's thought here as structured according to five questions, but I see Paul's logic as entailing four discrete questions.

God is for us, who can be against us?' And that makes a difference, doesn't it? The God who is never defeated by evil but always uses evil for good, the God who can never be outflanked or surprised or wearied or perplexed – this God is for us.

Do you realize that God is for you in all that he is doing in this world right now, whatever that means for you at this time in your life? We are often confused and sinful and defeated. But God is at work for us. You can put your name right here in verse 31: 'God is for _____.' And if God is for you, then *God* would have to be defeated for *you* to be defeated.

Paul is asking unanswerable questions here, setting before us reasons for feeling loved by God. His second question is in verse 32: 'He who did not spare his own Son but gave him up for us all, how will he not also with him graciously give us all things?' In other words, if God gave us his most generous gift at the cross, how could he possibly begrudge us anything else? Is he going to nickel-and-dime us now? We may wonder how far will God go with us. At what point might God say, 'I'm fed up with you. The deal's off'? What is the extent, the very outer limit, of God's love for you and me?

Before the foundation of the world, in eternity past, when God was framing his eternal decrees, he did not say, 'I will love them by giving them a fruitful creation, splendid bodies, keen minds, happy children, meaningful tasks. But I will not part with my Son for them. That's asking too much, especially for them. Nobody gets my Son.' God did not say that. It is not in his heart to be that way. God is rich in mercy, and God is a big spender. He delivered up his own Son for us all. Therefore, God's love for you has no outer limit! We are the ones who measure out our love in a calculating way, pennies at a time, always careful not to give away too much. But God does not love that way. God is glorified by lavishing his mercies upon us without regard for the cost to himself.

So what are these 'all things' that God will surely give us, since he has gone so far as to give up his Son for us all? 'All things' are presumably all the incremental steps it is going to take to get us from where we are now to where God has promised we will be forever – with Christ, like Christ, in heaven. So if we have Christ at all, we stand to inherit *all* that God can give to undeserving sinners. 'No eye has seen, no ear has heard, no mind has conceived what God has prepared for those who love him' (1 Corinthians 2:9, NIV).

But again, look at the way Paul asks the question. He does not simply ask, 'Will not God give us all things?' If he had asked that question, we might have replied, 'Well, I can think of a lot of things God hasn't given me. I have unmet needs. I have unanswered prayers.' But that is why Paul asks the question in light of the cross of God's Son. Yes, we do suffer deprivation in this life. But God wants us to know that he withholds nothing that we need to become like Christ and to live forever with Christ. God takes a bold, 'whatever-it-takes' attitude toward you and me. He stands ready to give us whatever we need to be prepared for heaven.

Do you see something else here in verse 32? Paul just takes it for granted that God's greatest gift of love to us is his Son. We do not take that for granted. We do not prize Christ as God prizes Christ – the greatest gift of love that could possibly be given. What gifts do we want from God? We want a new job, a new car, a new marriage, whatever. And when God does not give us what we want, we feel unloved and we pout and complain. But the problem is not a failure in God. The problem is that we have devalued Christ. We have arranged our affections so that, to us, a new job is more to be desired, more to be sought after, more to be rejoiced over, than possessing the Son of God. But Paul could write Romans

8:32 because his affections were so arranged that he gladly
suffered the loss of all things that he might gain Christ
(Philippians 3:7-8). If we want to feel loved by God, we must
repent that we have disrelished God's greatest gift and plead
with him that from the heart we would esteem Christ above
all else. That way, having him, we know we already have
God's best. We know he is going to throw in everything else
we need to enjoy his greatest gift fully. And that is when we
stop feeling sorry for ourselves and start to feel loved.

Paul's third question is in verses 33-34: 'Who will bring
any charge against God's elect? It is God who justifies. Who
is to condemn? Christ Jesus is the one who died – more than
that, who was raised – who is at the right hand of God, who
indeed is interceding for us.' God considers our case closed,
in our favor, not because he has lowered his standards or has
lost the stomach for punishment, but because the justice of
his law has been satisfied for us at the cross. And now the
Son intercedes for us to affirm the Father's mercies. The Holy
Spirit intercedes through us within (verse 26), and Jesus
intercedes for us above (verse 34). We have not a dead Jesus
but a living Jesus, raised from the dead, and not just a living
Jesus but a glorified Jesus, at the right hand of God. And we
are always on his heart. We have no problem too great, or
too small, for him to solve. We have no sin too dirty for him
to cleanse. His compassion is always upon us, and he is able
to see us all the way through to glory. Your sin cannot keep
you from your glory, because your sin is what your interceding
Priest removes.

So if the Father has chosen us and justified us and the Son
is interceding for us, who is going to win a case against us?
Who is going to get around the cross by appealing to a higher
court? God *is* the supreme court of the universe. We cannot
be de-justified, so that we find ourselves under condemnation
again. Why? Because God the Father and God the Son have

done all that God can do to establish us forever with perfect righteousness in his sight.

Of course, the devil wants us to *feel* condemned. For him, a good day is dragging us down into despair over our sins. Even our own hearts accuse us, whispering to us that people like us have no right to enjoy God, that we deserve to be miserable Christians, that the only right thing is to live forever under the cloud of our sins, that it would be hypocritical to enjoy God's love, that such grace is cheap grace and that we have to pay our dues, and so on. And there is a half-truth in there, we do deserve to be miserable. But in Christ, God gives us what we do not deserve. What sin does the cross fail to overrule? Our Savior raises his wounded hands over us, and our Judge confirms that Christ's merit has indeed compensated fully for all our guilt forever. The case is closed. And we move on, rejoicing!

Paul's last unanswerable question is found in verse 35: 'Who shall separate us from the love of Christ?' Paul looks around and sees what we see, all the enemies of our happiness in Christ, and he defies them to tear us from the loving grip of Christ. So what would have to happen to prove that Christ no longer loved us, that he had abandoned us? Paul throws out some possibilities: 'Shall trouble or hardship or persecution or famine or nakedness or danger or sword?' That's a realistic assessment of life, isn't it? Stress, opposition, unmet needs, danger, violence – that is life. That is life for Christians. And Paul does not deny or even minimize it. In fact, he draws upon Psalm 44 to remind us how brutal life can be – the flock of God herded to the slaughter: 'As it is written, 'For your sake we are being killed all the day long; we are regarded as sheep to be slaughtered'' (verse 36). The world as one vast slaughterhouse – what a perspective! It is not pretty, but it does match the facts, because God's people do suffer. And they cannot always make sense of it – that is the whole point of Psalm 44, which Paul is quoting here. The people of God are living for the Lord and trying to do his will. And yet 'for your sake' – because of God, not in spite of him – they suffer.

But the gospel opens up to us an underlying truth that makes all the difference, in verses 37-39:

> But[3] in all [not in some, but in all] these things we are more than conquerors through him who loved us. For I am convinced that neither death nor life, neither angels nor demons, neither the present nor the future, nor any powers, neither height nor depth, nor anything else in all creation, will be able to separate us from the love of God that is in Christ Jesus our Lord.

Do you see what Paul is doing? He *wants* us to see all our enemies swirling around us. He *wants* us to imagine the worst case scenario. He *wants* us to ask the tough questions, to see if the love of God remains credible even then. And he admits, Yes, life beats us up. We get bloodied along the way. But in it all, there is a love that will not let us go. God's love will not allow our faith to die, because his love undergirds our faith. Our faith may lie there on the ground and bleed and twitch for a while. But we get up again and trust God again and go on. Satan pours all hell out on our heads, and we do not respond bitterly, 'I will never trust God again. What a fool I was to open my heart to him. I'm making my own way from now on!' No. We waver. We weep. We agonize. But we get back up again and say, 'I will trust God. He must have

---

3. The ESV translates, 'No, in all these things . . .,' presumably construing verse 37 as Paul's reply to the questions of verse 35. I would rather translate literally, with the NASB, 'But in all these things . . .,' lest the English translation give the impression that verse 37 is correcting the assessment of human life chillingly, and correctly, set forth in verse 36.

a good reason for this. I will go on with God.' Why do we do this? Why don't we give up on God? Because God loves us. His love created our faith. His love undergirds our faith. His love is deepening our faith. And he is going to bring us by our faith through all our afflictions, more like Christ and more fit to be with Christ.

Certainty in the love of God is how the gospel makes heroes out of ordinary sinners. Life is mean. It is hard to bear. But real life does not mean that God no longer cares. In it all, we move forward not as victims but as victors, because everything happening to us, while not necessarily good in itself, is working for our good and is guided by God's love. The love of God is the key to the narrative of our lives. Your life is a love story! So stop thinking of yourself as a victim. You are more than a victor. Your real life just happens to be the vehicle God is using to bring you to splendor. Your sufferings do not define you; the love of God defines you. And your persevering confidence in this love *is* the overwhelming victory of Romans 8:37.

So in this passage Paul asks four revealing questions and declares four stabilizing declarations: God sticks up for us, God provides for us, God justifies us, God loves us. God's love is loyal, generous, just and eternal. God fights for us, God gives to us, God defends us, God cares for us – no matter what happens. God is for us in friendship, God is over us in provision, God is around us in protection, God is with us in preservation. Therefore, we should never feel opposed by God, we should never feel deprived by God, we should never feel condemned by God and we should never feel abandoned by God. We may so believe the gospel that we live in the atmosphere of God's overcoming partnership, God's over-compensating generosity, God's overruling advocacy and God's overwhelming love.

Maybe you have not been feeling loved by God. But God

never promised that nothing would ever separate us from our earthly comforts. God never promised that life would be fair. Let's look for God's love where he himself has promised it. Nothing can ever separate us from the love of God *in Christ Jesus our Lord*! And what is his love? To make us more like Christ, and to prepare us to live forever with Christ. *That* is the love of God, from which nothing can separate us. If we set our hearts upon that prize, we *will* feel loved. And we will go up against beasts and demons, as the Roman Christians in fact did, totally convinced that God's love will overcome it all.

Robert Bruce, the seventeenth-century Scottish minister, came to breakfast one morning with his family. He sat in silence. But suddenly he said to his daughter next to him, 'Hold, daughter, hold; my Master calls me.' He asked for a Bible, but he was dying and his eyesight failed him. 'Cast me up the eighth of Romans,' and he repeated the words as his daughter read to him: 'I am sure that nothing in all creation will be able to separate us from the love of God in Christ Jesus our Lord.' 'God be with you, my children. I have breakfasted with you, and shall sup with my Lord Jesus this night.' And putting his hand on the page of Romans 8, he said, 'I die, believing these words.'[4]

What do *you* say in response to Romans 8? Won't you say something like this? 'Nothing will ever separate me from the love of God in Christ Jesus my Lord. All my hope for happiness is secure in God's salvation through Christ. He doesn't give this gift only to take it back later on. He is committed to me, come what may, now and forever. Therefore, no more uncertainty for me! By God's grace, I will live and I will die, believing these words.' And armed

4. Cf. Marcus L. Loane, *The Hope of Glory* (Waco, 1968), page 160.

with that powerful faith, let us demonstrate the transforming power of the gospel in our communities and around the world, for God's greater glory, our richer joy and the salvation of the nations!

Raymond C. Ortlund Jr serves as Senior Minister at First Presbyterian Church, Augusta, Georgia, USA. He was formerly Professor of Old Testament at Trinity Evangelical Divinity School in Deerfield, Illinois. His PhD is from the University of Aberdeen, Scotland.